THE SECRET REBELLION

THE SECRET REBELLION

DANIEL OSIGBE

Matador
9 Priory Business Park,
Wistow Road, Kibworth Beauchamp,
Leicestershire. LE8 0RX
Tel: (+44) 116 279 2299
Fax: (+44) 116 279 2277
Email: books@troubador.co.uk
Web: www.troubador.co.uk/matador

ISBN 978 178088 284 0

British Library Cataloguing in Publication Data.
A catalogue record for this book is available from the British Library.

Typeset by Troubador Publishing Ltd, Leicester, UK

Matador is an imprint of Troubador Publishing Ltd

Printed and bound in the UK by TJ International, Padstow, Cornwall

In Loving memory of
Donald Osigbe

CONTENTS

FOREWORD

This masterpiece by Dr Daniel Osigbe, my mentee, is not a book that should be treated with a "brush-through" reading pace. It is a book that provokes one's hidden inner strength and resistance to temptation and its resultant effect from Rebellion.

The author's description of "what rebellion is" is unraveled through a combination of a beautiful well-crafted plot set in the beautiful Island of Ireland with a touch of the English culture but culminating into a straight message of what God hates, and that is Rebellion!

Daniel's book is a must read and should be read with a pragmatic approach in discussing the effects rebellion could potentially have on us as we journey with the Lord as created beings who should know and do better especially when we know the Lord Jesus Christ.

The author's emphasis on purity seems to be the main weapon against rebellion deducted from the chapters in his book as he lays great layers on the foundation we build upon in our daily activities as children of the Lord. He goes on to advise us to take heed to be humble and do

God's bidding decrying rebellion from our lives and I do agree.

I do recommend this book to all including the secular world and the saints of the Kingdom of Heaven.

I give my blessings to you Dr Daniel Osigbe and salute you for this masterpiece.

Dr Douglas Adjepong (Minister)
Trinity Baptist Church, UK
Founder of Revival Prayers Ministry and Leadership
& Mentoring Academy

INTRODUCTION

There has been news of a universal revolt. A revolt that has spread from the hearts of men into the home, into society and now pervades even our government. As a result of this revolt against God there has been a catastrophic breakdown in affairs on earth. Things are out of sync with one another, no longer following their original plans, but now they are at war even within themselves. This conflict has infiltrated into their relationships, their every-day lives and the justice of their government. It stays true however that there remains but one hope for them all. Who will reveal it to them that there is only one who can bring reconciliation and resolution to the conflict that rages even in the secret parts of the earth.

Let us hear what God has to say about this age old rebellion, that is worsening in our age.

Zephaniah 3
New International Version (NIV)

Jerusalem
¹ Woe to the city of oppressors,
rebellious and defiled!

² She obeys no one,
she accepts no correction.
    She does not trust in the LORD,
    she does not draw near to her God.
³ Her officials within her
    are roaring lions;
    her rulers are evening wolves,
    who leave nothing for the morning.
⁴ Her prophets are unprincipled;
    they are treacherous people.
    Her priests profane the sanctuary
    and do violence to the law.
⁵ The LORD within her is righteous;
    he does no wrong.
    Morning by morning he dispenses his justice,
    and every new day he does not fail,
    yet the unrighteous know no shame.

Jerusalem Remains Unrepentant

⁶ "I have destroyed nations;
    their strongholds are demolished.
    I have left their streets deserted,
    with no one passing through.
    Their cities are laid waste;
    they are deserted and empty.
⁷ Of Jerusalem I thought,
    'Surely you will fear me
    and accept correction!'
    Then her place of refuge[a] would not be destroyed,
    nor all my punishments come upon[b] her.

But they were still eager
to act corruptly in all they did.
[8] Therefore wait for me,"
declares the LORD,
"for the day I will stand up to testify.[c]
I have decided to assemble the nations,
to gather the kingdoms
and to pour out my wrath on them—
all my fierce anger.
The whole world will be consumed
by the fire of my jealous anger.

Restoration of Israel's Remnant

[9] "Then I will purify the lips of the peoples,
that all of them may call on the name of the LORD
and serve him shoulder to shoulder.
[10] From beyond the rivers of Cush[d]
my worshipers, my scattered people,
will bring me offerings.
[11] On that day you, Jerusalem, will not be put to shame
for all the wrongs you have done to me,
because I will remove from you
your arrogant boasters.
Never again will you be haughty
on my holy hill.
[12] But I will leave within you
the meek and humble.
The remnant of Israel
will trust in the name of the LORD.
[13] They will do no wrong;

they will tell no lies.
A deceitful tongue
will not be found in their mouths.
They will eat and lie down
and no one will make them afraid."

[14] *Sing, Daughter Zion;*
shout aloud, Israel!
Be glad and rejoice with all your heart,
Daughter Jerusalem!

[15] *The LORD has taken away your punishment,*
he has turned back your enemy.
The LORD, the King of Israel, is with you;
never again will you fear any harm.

[16] *On that day*
they will say to Jerusalem,
"Do not fear, Zion;
do not let your hands hang limp.

[17] *The LORD your God is with you,*
the Mighty Warrior who saves.
He will take great delight in you;
in his love he will no longer rebuke you,
but will rejoice over you with singing."

[18] *"I will remove from you*
all who mourn over the loss of your appointed
festivals, which is a burden and reproach for you.

[19] *At that time I will deal*
with all who oppressed you.
I will rescue the lame;
I will gather the exiles.
I will give them praise and honour

in every land where they have suffered shame.
²⁰ *At that time I will gather you;*
   at that time I will bring you home.
   I will give you honour and praise
   among all the peoples of the earth
   when I restore your fortunes[e]
   before your very eyes,"
   says the LORD.

CHAPTER 1

The Secret Rebellion – Origins

It all started so small, as the little Jonah was very much a perfect young man. He did everything his master wanted him to do, he was industrious, hardworking, and under his hand his master's business had actually prospered. The logging business was booming, there were large businesses from Asia and important tradesmen from the Americas all vying for his service.

Jonah was a good looking young man, aged twenty-three years, six foot and of a muscular build. He lived on the estate, where he worked. There were around 800 cows, 300 sheep's, 120 chicken and 60 pigs on average that were kept in the estate in an average year. This was the average number of animals that were brought up in the ranch and sold for profit on a yearly basis.

His parents were Irish, born and raised in the city of Limerick, Ireland. This might be of some significance, who can tell; the city known as 'City of the Violated Treaty'. At this time Ireland had not yet been partitioned. They had only one son and decided to move down to England because of the unrest between the Catholics and Protestants. They themselves were Protestant, but not so religiously inclined. The year was 1830 when they made the move to England, by chance or call it fate they ended up in the town of Stafford where they raised their young son. It certainly was a change moving from the 'Cathair of Limerick' to the 'Baile of Stafford'.

Limerick was the third largest city of Ireland, and the capital city of the county Limerick, a city situated on several curves and islands of the river Shannon, before progressing into an estuary. Limerick was a place that could often sidetrack you, especially if you were a young man. Jonah had been through some tough times in life but somehow he had always made it through. Though he had indeed come from humble beginnings, and his parents didn't always have much they had always managed to feed him. Somehow he managed to stay on track.

It is important to understand our Origins
Seven days was all it took
Even a day less
For man to be
And your future determined

It was His thoughts
The Creator's hands
Spoken before time
That time should bring you forth

Not of your will
Yet dust of dust
Clay of the soil
Beautiful in workmanship
A testament to the Creator.

The Estate owner

The estate owner's name was Logan,

"Jonah, my boy! Come, I've something to share with you. The coal season is here, I'm thinking of diversifying. You see, coal is as always an important commodity, and if you have been keeping up with the news they've recently discovered coal in neighbouring Cannock. We can make a killing in this market and yes, you'll definitely have higher wages".

"Yes master, I will find out all the information we need, I'll source the buyers and make sure we secure our supply of coal."

"Jonah, you are the best, and since you've been here our business has tripled its profits".

This was one of many conversations that the estate owner had with Jonah over the many years, and the outcome was always the same, success! Jonah was excited, he loved working on these projects and seeing them through to the end, for maybe one day he might be seeing through his own projects with all the profits going to him. "One day" might be the inception of Jonah's own success. Unknown to Jonah, there were many forces out there ready to offer him just what he thought he needed.

He had dreamt of owning his own ranch one day, he thought it would be nice for him to have his own animals, his own contracts, his own empire; then he could also have the perfect family he wanted. How was he to know that his wish was about to be granted? For now, he had to settle with bringing his master's vision to fulfilment. Jonah had been apprenticed to Logan since he was fifteen years of age by his parents, since that time he had earned their upkeep. Logan had recently installed a sawmill on the ranch as their profit margin widened and they had recruited a few more workers.

Jonah had moved out of his parent's home in Stafford to live with Logan on the ranch. He was well known for his industry and everybody liked him. He could be seen tending the flock, feeding the horses and after a hard day's work, he would go off into town to negotiate with Logan's business associates. He mainly delivered timber on his horse-drawn cart on the weekends and on Wednesdays; he was very reputable for his punctuality. Jonah was so busy that he hardly had time to see his family, to a large extent he had become part of Logan's family and ate at the table with everybody at the ranch. Logan had in truth committed all the daily runnings of the ranch into Jonah's hands.

Many are the thoughts of a man's heart but it's the Lord's counsel that will prevail. From time to time we have our own ideas; in fact we are gods, creating our ideas, with the ability to bring it through. We also receive divine ideas and divine instructions from time to time, the fulfilment of which gives great joy and satisfaction. When we are busy doing our master's business, we have little time for our ideas, but when we are idle the pull and strength of our ideas encourages us to bring to pass our own vision. In truth the inception of our idea takes form, it is with great pride that we see our dreams come to life. We become filled with the realization that "I can do, I can accomplish, I forethought and it was done", and our conclusion becomes, "I am brilliant, I am super", and our subconscious says "surely I am like unto God".

Recently there had been news of a rich foreigner who had come to neighbouring Stone, and bought a large piece of land. Rumour had it that he was very rich and it appeared that his intent was to break into the logging and farming market. The year was 1846, the logging business was still booming, timber trade was on the upswing. And in those times British timber was highly desired. Edgar had brought with him a big reputation; all he needed was a very skilled man who understood the market. His policy rested on the theory of selective logging of high quality trees.

The Rich foreigner

The threat of war with England had passed, whereas the war with the Mexicans raged on. Slavery was dying out but the spirit of enterprise was rife. In the plain country of Massachusetts lived Edgar. His family were migrants themselves, they had migrated from Ireland, but the same could be said for most people in New England. Edgar had become successful purely from his innovation in business and his amazing drive.

Sure enough, America was on the up, there was interest in the modern forms of painting and artistry. However Edgar had concentrated on an industry that was old but was at the same time experiencing a boom. His family had been into the logging business, Edgar had been able to build mills and as a recent spin off, the printing branch of the business.

He supplied timber to various industries, including the building industry, the printing industry as well as local farms and local industries. Edgar had become one of the many successful entrepreneurs in this new America. However he had been urged by his relatives to join them in England. He had resisted these urges for many years, but by now he was getting fed up of it, and he had heard of the booming logging business in England. He responded by sending a telegraph to his relatives in Great Britain to expect him shortly.

As for Jonah, he would never betray his master, his skills and entrepreneurship were sufficient to make him finish the task at hand. He managed to secure contracts from the landowners with coal mines, with great ease he manoeuvred himself in to positions where all the merchants and tradesmen were begging for his service. On one such meeting he met Edgar.

"Are you Logan's tradesman?" Edgar enquired

"Yes I am sir, and you are Edgar, well known for your shrewdness in business."

"You have learnt well. I suppose I could not expect any less from Logan's trusted man. Logan is a very intelligent man, very apt at accumulating wealth. He has done excellently in securing your services. How does he fare?"

"He is well sir! Very much indeed, he is much beloved by the country folks here, from Stafford to Shropshire, and here I am in Cannock extending his reach even further. There have been some maligning folks who have accused him of trying to monopolize the market. Though, I would say not, but that he knows how to take care of his stars. Forgive I pray, the length of my speech." "You sure are a fine young man," said Edgar, "I've heard of you. I say I would be tempted, but never mind."

"I do not understand, explain please."

"Since it has crossed my mind, I suppose I had did better tell you, what do you say?"

"Very well so, if you must."

"I've been watching you for some time, while you bargained, and I thought if you didn't have an employer, I have the idea of making you your own boss, I mean I felt you were skilful and if you had your own business you and I can make a fortune!"

"Where has this idea come from?" replied Jonah with a slight stammer.

"We're just imagining here. In this world I could give you a an estate, your own. The coal industry is just kicking up and the logging business is still in boom; you do business on your terms, your plans, your ideas, on your ranch, and I get 15% of what you make, but of course everything is yours." Edgar finished his statement with a wry smile, almost like he knew his offer connected with something deep in Jonah's mind.

"Your offer is tempting, but the contract with my master is binding." Jonah replied hesitantly.

"Let me know when you make the decision. Remember we were just thinking and this would only be the case if you were not Logan's right hand man"

(Starts to walk away, and then turns back) "Or would it?"

The Idea

Did God really say that you should not eat of this fruit? For He knows that if you would eat of the fruit of this tree, that you would be like Him, you shall not die? When the enemy comes to speak into our lives, he doesn't usually come directly in contradicting the things of God, but he raises a question. He causes us to question the things of God, "did God really say that you shouldn't, did God really say you should". And when we start to pay attention to the voice of the enemy we become unsure of the things that God has spoken to us. Adam was not deceived like Eve was but ate the fruit of the tree for his wife's sake. At that point of his temptation he should have hearkened to the voice of God rather than the voice of his wife. I've found myself at times doing the exact opposite of what God said despite knowing what he said, because of affections I had for myself, towards others I care about and even other gods (money, Television, women, luxury etc).

When we are tempted we are drawn away by our own lust, enticed by our own desires. "When tempted, no one should say, 'God is tempting me.' For God cannot be tempted by evil, nor does he tempt anyone;" (James 1;13).

"Master Logan, I have something to say to you. The

8

business has prospered and your reach is great. You've done this by yourself and your ingenuity has brought you this far. I have been thinking that you don't need me to be here anymore, there are more capable men than me. I think at this point I want to start on my own project, I want to carve out something for myself, I want to make my own mark in the world." In saying all this, Jonah was unable to look Logan in the face, but kept his head bowed low, and he had a distant look in his eyes. Almost like he wasn't there; but rather his ghost.

This saying greatly vexed Logan the ranch master and grieved his soul. And Logan asked "from where has this thought come from? Who have you spoken to, for you are still under a binding contract?" You could see the age lines on Logan's face, lines of anguish.

"I was offered an opportunity to own my own estate, to run my own business and to publish my own ideas."

To which Logan replied with a hint of exasperation "you have more than you need here, all that and more, and I have been like a father to you. What more are you looking for?"

"I'm sorry master," Jonah replied tamely.

This was met with a shout from Logan, "you know better than me, that I am no longer your master, the decision was yours." Logan felt as though a part of him just died.

"So my convention and organisations are of little worth to you. I would have preferred you to stay but if you must leave, you can leave. What you say sounds good, it is funny that you never realized that all that you asked for you already have, you were already your own master, but in my eyes you've traded your freedom in my house to serve another taskmaster. You have broken the bond of our contract."

So Jonah moved to Shrewsbury with all that he had; he had his own ranch, he ran coal from Cannock to Wolverhampton, and ran a mill in the midst of Stafford, not too far from Stafford castle. In those times trade was good. He settled in a nice cottage off the road that was to become evolution road in times that were to come. The weeks turned to months, the months lengthened into years and in 3 good years Jonah had become a very rich man. His estate was as large as that of his former master, and he had become as successful in less time. Figuratively speaking he had seized his opportunity at the right time. He even got married to the beautiful Eleanor who was cousin to the countess of the castle. He had many links with the palace, he knew many of the noble men and merchants and in those days business was good, and life was great. Besides he was only getting started, at this rate all of Stafford, Cannock, Shrewsbury, Shropshire came under his trading influence, he had proved his master wrong.

Jonah was a very distinguished man indeed, well respected and sought after. He often entertained visitors in his front room, more often than not they were business partners or men who wanted to discuss some business of some sort with him. He dressed distinctly, he had a 3 piece suit, a navy blue waistcoat and dark overalls, and now walked with a stick, not that he needed one; but it gave him some character.

He was often seen pacing down the enigmatic streets of Shropshire, on his daily rounds to oversee the different businesses he was in charge of. In truth Edgar had been true to his word and had not interfered one bit, all he did was reap the benefits and provide the overall direction, Edgar and the surrounding towns truly believed Jonah was a man with a vision.

(Six months into the third year after, Jonah left his first master)

Logan was sailing down the river Severn, the waters were quiet but the sky was grey and red. He said to his new right hand man "it looks as though a storm is coming this way".

Joey said, huh, it appears so. Joey was a big fellow, not too bright but not dull either, not bad looking but not handsome in any description of the word. He wanted to make it to the other side of the shore quickly. He remembered they still had to make their way to Wolverhampton by road, almost 17 miles down the track. At least they will be on a boat; it was much faster than riding there by horse, which would take twice as long. Business had been steady, no significant growth in the last few years, it appears the larger share of the market available had been claimed by Jonah and his new financier and it didn't appear as if there were any prospects of claiming it back.

Logan was satisfied though, his business and empire hadn't really grown in the last few years but he thought he was in a state of equilibrium. The share of the market

Jonah had peeled away with him when he left, he had regained in the new customers he gained; he had learnt to apply a different marketing ploy. Unknown to Jonah, in his eyes Jonah had more than just left his estate; he had indeed picked at the fabric of his own heart. Outwardly he had let Jonah go easily, but for a long time his heart and mind were in turmoil. For he had considered Jonah a son, though clearly Jonah was no son, at least that was clearer now. For a son always remained in the house, and everything the father owned belonged to the son.

It was the first Tuesday, the 7th day of the month, that Jonah received the news that brought his world crashing down, in another time this couldn't have been possible, in fact it was outrageous. Edgar visited him at 12 noon; he told him he had very difficult news for him. He had recently lost his father who lived with his mother in the Americas, in New England. Yet that wasn't the worst news for Jonah, if not for the fact that as a result Edgar was moving to New England to be closer to his mother. He was selling up everything he had and had no intentions of coming back. As Edgar said blood is thicker than water. He assured him, you will be able to cope, the resources are within you, and you will find something profitable to do. Edgar left by the end of the week. On the Saturday morning he sailed for New England. He had found a buyer, the name of the buyer he had not disclosed to Jonah.

The result was that Jonah was left without a job, no wage, no pay, and no profit. All he had by the end of the week was the very roof he and his wife slept under. This was the parting gift that Edgar had left for Jonah. That afternoon Jonah learnt that the new owner was Logan his former master, who now had control of all the industries in that region of midland England. He had a monopoly on the coal mines, the cotton factory; the logging business and most of the farming and cattle rearing land was now his. In Jonah's estimation Logan was now one of the richest men in England. As Jonah sat in the fields outside his home, the clouds finally let up, and the sky pelted rain. In the midst of the thunder and sodden ground Jonah trudged back into his house unsure of how to explain to his wife how they had lost everything. It was a shame to see Jonah's head hung low, even he had become just as all the ordinary men in Stafford. Just before he entered the house, his pipe fell from his hand and stayed on the ground, his status lost in the mud.

All that roamed in his mind were thoughts of the past, sailing logs across the Severn river. What a twist in his tale, where he thought he was his own master he was only a servant. Where he reckoned he was no more than a servant, he was actually a master, but just not his own master.

Be not deceived
For whatever a man soweth, so shall he reap
He tells his friends a story
But time will tell a different story

Where he once taught himself
Vindicated in the eyes of his friends
Time judged him and proved him wrong
Now all he can afford

Is a broken spirit
He must needs realise
That what he needs most
Is a contrite heart
Not what he possessed before

CHAPTER 2

The Cold War

There is an ongoing war, but the outcome is already pre-determined. There is also an age-old rebellion, and this rebellion has already been judged. Ever since man was removed from the garden of Eden and men have multiplied on the face of the earth, as people have filled the earth, even so has this rebellion grown in the hearts of men, and its manifestations has multiplied in the world and throughout time. It is a rebellion that started in the heart and grows in secret, in the dark. We have seen its manifestation at different times since the world began, and in different ways.

This ongoing war is not about which is the strongest side or who would get lucky in battle and win the war. Strangely enough the victor is already known, what is important for us to understand is which side we would choose. Would we choose to side with God or side with the devil, who is the father of the first rebellion and every rebellion afterwards against God almighty?

There is a secret rebellion because we're at war and we're on the winning side. There is open warfare, but there is also a secret warfare of the enemy. 'The cold war' was the ideological confrontation between the Soviet Union and Western powers. The Cold War *(Kholodnaya voyna which is the Russian translation*, 1947–1991) was the continuing state of political conflict, military tension, proxy wars, and economic competition existing after World War II (1939–1945) between the Communist World – primarily the Soviet Union and its satellite states and allies – and the powers of the Western world, primarily the United States and its allies. Although the main participants, military force was never officially used directly, the conflict was expressed through military coalitions, strategic conventional force deployments, extensive aid to states deemed vulnerable, espionage, propaganda, conventional and nuclear arms races, appeals to neutral nations, rivalry at sports events, and technological competitions such as the Space Race.

I explore the idea of the cold war because throughout its duration there was never any direct military action between the communist world and the Western world. However there was a state of antagonism, this is synonymous to an extent to the idea I'm trying to portray regarding the secret rebellion. The difference being that the cold war was a tactical fight for supremacy which the United States and its allies won as the Soviet economy stagnated and started to collapse. However in our case the Kingdom of God is already victorious.

The victory of the Kingdom of heaven is assured and final; despite this, the agents of the Kingdom of darkness propagate and wage a secret war to cause many souls to be lost and in the underlying hope that they will have the victory one day. Their attempts are mainly to deceive human hearts and minds, as the Almighty God is not deceived. They attempt to corrupt many, they make corrupt men wicked, they make atheists idolators and cause the slothful to become lovers of themselves. Their one rule is evil, corruption and anything sinister, employing the twisting of truth to even confound those that think that they are saved.

The war they wage is more effective when it's secret otherwise they would have no problem with it coming to light. And we know that light overcomes darkness, darkness vanishes at the entrance of light. The power of the messages they propagate is the fact that it is propagated in secret and from secret places, so that the hearts of men who have not satisfied themselves with the truth of 'Christ Jesus' might wander from the truth. They stand no chance if their works were to be revealed in the light. We can see scriptural warning in this. We're warned that times will come when people will call what is evil good, and what is good evil.

"Woe to those who call evil good and good evil, who put darkness for light and light for darkness, who put bitter for sweet and sweet for bitter."
(Isaiah Ch.5 vv20)

Today in our world it's fast becoming the trend that those that speak against issues such as homosexuality are labelled as violating human freedom and rights. Yet it is such doctrines that keep the souls and hearts of men bound in the prisons of darkness and in a path that leads to hell. In today's world, the norms and values of Western civilization scorn the teachings and order of God, advocating that people should not be discouraged from giving their bodies to un-natural use. They call sexual promiscuity freedom, and cover sodomy with the idea that everyone is different. A phrase that can be used is 'whatever rocks your boat'.

The government outlaws the rightful disciplining of our children, it is approximated to child cruelty. Yet we see the full result of this in that we have children who are becoming uncontrollable, we have broken down family units and a malfunctioning in the society, with the appearing of many varieties of social, spiritual and natural vagrants from that which is natural to man. Many of us come from societies in which we were physically disciplined, those of us who are older who were even brought up in this society were also physically disciplined. We know it didn't do us any harm but rather good, as it shaped our character and attitudes.

We can see the trap that the enemy sets for society; here the government will cite cases of child abuse. In citing these cases, they move on to twisting and manipulating the reality of this cases to say that there is a great danger of most children being abused if physical disciplining of children is allowed. The first thing to note is that they have lost the distinction between what is good and what is bad, physical abuse is perpetuated by criminals. However just as a shepherd beats the sheep to guide them in a safe direction, it is the same way that children are physically disciplined that they take a safe direction. I would postulate that this provides part of the reason why so many young people today are not walking in the right direction in life.

> "Whoever spares the rod hates their children, but the one who loves their children is careful to discipline them".
>
> (Proverbs Ch.13 vv24)

This scripture verse tells us that if we love our children we would actually discipline them many times, as it portrays parents whose desire it is to see their children grow up morally sound and to have good character.

Looking at the riots in the summer of 2011, that took place on the weekend preceding and on the 4th of August, many people suggested different reasons for how the young people could have reached such a state where they were unafraid of parents and now that they are unafraid of the state. The young rioters demonstrated with impunity, attacking police, vandalising shops and stealing. It wasn't just government properties they destroyed; they burnt people's businesses, and robbed people's homes, attacked innocent bystanders who were not partaking in the riots. During this period of rioting there were at least five deaths which were directly attributed to the riots and the events surrounding it.

I conducted a small survey among a group of young teenagers based at a youth group in Croydon, London, which was one of the cities at the heart of the London riots. Essentially I asked them 'why they think the London riots happened, here are some of their responses.

What do you think caused the London riots?

- Lack of discipline, domino effect

- It was an excuse for people to get free goods. They were called London riots but the only place that actually had a riot was Tottenham. Everything else was just an excuse for criminality

- Youth acting out and following others mindlessly

- People saw it as an opportunity to get free stuff and thought they would get away with it. They saw Tottenham rioting and looting and wanted to do the same.

- They happened because the police shot Mark Duggan even though he didn't have a weapon in his hand. So the riots happened because the police force is seen as racist!

- I think the riots happened because of less youth facilities, government cut downs and break-down in families

- I think the riots happened because of anger and frustration with the government not providing enough for the community

- I think the riots happened because it was just something to do

- I think the riots happened because people saw it as an opportunity to take things for free and cause chaos.

The riots spread from town to town, then from city to city, showing no sign of quenching until it was met by force from the authorities. It started in Tottenham, London, possibly over the unexplained shooting by police of a young black man who was allegedly wielding a gun in a vehicle. The next day the gangs came out as well as every other unruly youth who wanted to riot, and they terrorized the streets from Brixton, to Hackney,

Peckham to Clapham, Woolwich to Croydon. Then it went to Bristol, Birmingham, and Manchester. And to think that as there was not one single person organizing this, how could people agree and have their minds set on one thing so quickly when it comes to destruction? Yet, do we allow rebellion to carry on in our hearts? In our churches?

Just as in the previous London riots of 1981 and 1985, many people voiced their opinion on what could have brought about such violent disorder in England among the youth. Some suggested it was due to the despairing state of the economy, others that it was due to perceived dissatisfaction with the police by various ethnic sectors of the community, some think it's due to increased tuition fees and lack of adequate provision for young people. The prime minister concluded there is a moral breakdown in our society. What is clear is that whatever view you might take on the actual cause, this problem didn't start in one day, but perhaps it's a consequence of hearts that have become rebellious and at the slightest opportunity seek anarchy, not considering the effects of everyone being a law unto themselves regarding all matters.

This example highlights how easy and quickly rebellious people can gather followers. Could it be that the condition of their hearts are all the same, so it is easy for them to follow one another into any rebellious cause? They didn't need to call a conference, they certainly were not part of a union, but they joined themselves together to become a vehicle of destruction. Mobile phones and social networking media played a large part in their organisation.

"22 Although they claimed to be wise, they became fools 23 and exchanged the glory of the immortal God for images made to look like a mortal human being and birds and animals and reptiles.

24 Therefore God gave them over in the sinful desires of their hearts to sexual impurity for the degrading of their bodies with one another. 25 They exchanged the truth about God for a lie, and worshipped and served created things rather than the Creator – who is forever praised. Amen.

26 Because of this, God gave them over to shameful lusts. Even their women exchanged natural sexual relations for unnatural ones. 27 In the same way the men also abandoned natural relations with women and were inflamed with lust for one another. Men committed shameful acts with other men, and received in themselves the due penalty for their error.

28 Furthermore, just as they did not think it worth while to retain the knowledge of God, so God gave them over to a depraved mind, so that they do what ought not to be done. 29 They have become filled with every kind of wickedness, evil, greed and depravity. They are full of envy, murder, strife, deceit and malice. They are gossips, 30 slanderers, God-haters, insolent, arrogant and boastful; they invent ways of doing evil; they disobey their parents; 31 they have no understanding, no fidelity, no love, no mercy. 32 Although they know God's righteous decree that those who do such things deserve death, they not only continue to do these very things but also approve of those who practise them".

(Romans Ch.1 vv22 -32)

There are numerous examples today of this secret rebellion and war. We see it in organizations like 'Al qaeda', which do not use direct means of fighting. They do not confront their enemies. In my reasoning I'm not exactly sure who their enemy is or what their purpose is. Is it just Americans and the West, if it is so why do they commit suicide bombings and other such attacks in Muslim countries? They usually use many threats and state certain purposes of what they are trying to achieve, but I cannot see that they mean anybody else any good. They think only about themselves and their agenda and use unlawful and unconventional means to have their voices heard by causing chaos and destruction. They are radical villains, using terror as a political weapon, while sound reasoning would reveal that their aims would never be achieved if they continue as terrorists.

Al qaeda founded by Osama Bin Laden, has called for a global Jihad. As I've already asked, against whom is their so called 'holy war' (Jihad) directed? According to their vision, they want a break from all foreign interference/influence in Muslim countries and envision a global sharia (Islamic) law as they despise all man-made laws. Regardless of what their true mission might be, in the same way 'Satan' uses strategy to bring terrorism upon the world, and he is particularly angry at those that belong to God. This is spoken of clearly in scriptures.

"11 They triumphed over him
by the blood of the Lamb

and by the word of their testimony;
they did not love their lives so much
as to shrink from death.
12 Therefore rejoice, you heavens
and you who dwell in them!
But woe to the earth and the sea,
because the devil has gone down to you!
He is filled with fury,
because he knows that his time is short."

(Rev Ch.12 vv11-12)

And just as in the cold war, terrorist organizations wage a war using indirect means. We know that whenever the enemy wages a war directly against the church it always appears as if it's winning but he has already lost from the outset. The consequences of such direct confrontations are the creation of martyrs, of men and women of whom this world was not worthy of, a demonstration of the power of God; that confirms that God is actively at work in establishing His kingdom in the earth. When the enemy fights like this the church is strengthened, for when the church is threatened, she turns to her Bridegroom who is Omnipotent and omniscience and can do all things and in His anger doth thread down the winepress of His fury. For He goeth, into battle Himself and conquers and conquers till all be put under His feet and dominion.

CHAPTER 3

The Idea of Rebellion

"12 How you have fallen from heaven,
morning star, son of the dawn!
You have been cast down to the earth,
you who once laid low the nations!
13 You said in your heart,
'I will ascend to the heavens;
I will raise my throne
above the stars of God;
I will sit enthroned on the mount of assembly,
on the utmost heights of Mount Zaphon.[b]
14 I will ascend above the tops of the clouds;
I will make myself like the Most High."

Isaiah Ch14 vv12 – 14

The above scriptural passage gives us an insight into how rebellion manifests and progresses.

In the passage above Lucifer had a position; the bible states his position - 'Son of the morning'. Then we can see from the passage, how the Word of God, discovers the thoughts of Lucifer to himself and to us the reader. We can see that his thoughts were "I will ascend into heaven", so he wanted to go up higher, he wanted a higher position, greater esteem, more glory, more recognition, more visibility, more reverence, and more attribution. I would think it safe to say the higher you go the more belongs to you. He wanted more, but what was wrong with him wanting more? Well, remember I said the passage above started by stating Lucifer's position, place, authority, scope of reverence and esteem: his title was 'Son of the Morning'.

In Hebrews Ch.4 vv12, the bible tells us that the word of God reveals what is in the heart.

"For the word of God is alive and active. Sharper than any double-edged sword, it penetrates even to dividing soul and spirit, joints and marrow; it judges the thoughts and attitudes of the heart".

Yet he (Lucifer) desired in his thoughts to ascend above his status, his place, his niche, his purpose. God creates things for purpose and as such he places them in certain positions to achieve that purpose, to fulfil this purpose he gives them a niche, a realm, a place of operation. Lucifer tried to change the purpose for which God created him for, here we can start to see the beginning of his rebellion or in accordance with my writing so far, the beginning of his disagreement with God's purpose. I feel it is safe to say at this point, that disagreeing with God's word is rebellion.

Imagine the plant saying to God, I no longer want to provide food and bread for man to eat, but I am going to provide light for man to see by. As such I will ascend into space and shine. First thoughts are that it cannot produce light, and it cannot ascend or shine for that matter. God prepared it and equipped it for its purpose, but it is not equipped for the purpose it desired. Lucifer was not equipped for the place he desired. Rebellion is the desire or attempt to move beyond the capabilities that God has given to you. If I may give an example those that practice magic, mind control, witch craft are in rebellion. That's why the scripture says ' rebellion is as the sin of witchcraft and stubbornness as iniquity and idolatory... ' (1 Sam Ch.15 vv23)

Man was never made to control another man's mind, neither was power given unto him to control spiritual powers according to his own will. Rather God gave man dominion over all that he created on earth, and called man to be subject unto His will.

Examining the second part of verse 23, when we put it in plain English, the bible says stubbornness or in other words pride is wickedness and like unto worshipping an idol. A stubborn person is one who is resolutely adherent to his own ideas or desires, stubbornness is also defined as the trait of being difficult to handle or overcome. In the story of Lucifer, the idol was Lucifer, he esteemed himself above the purposes of God and as we are later to see, he esteemed himself like unto God. In the story of human pride, we esteem ourselves above the purposes for which God made us, and we worship ourselves, we worship our dreams, we worship our thoughts/ideas above God's Word and ideals. The story of rebellion begins with a heart of dissatisfaction and pride.

'I will exalt myself above the stars of God'. This phrase shows the other aspect of rebellion which is rooted in pride. The stars of God where higher than Lucifer, yet he thought to put himself over them, because he thought he was better, more beautiful than them. The scripture says promotion comes neither from the east or west but is of the Lord (Psalm Ch.75 vv6). The authority to exalt someone comes only from God, an attempt to do otherwise, is an attempt to usurp God's authority, if I looked at it from this point of view I can imagine why God says He is distant from the proud, but gives grace to the humble. In other words, He is distant from anyone who tries to usurp his authority but graceful to the meek, lowly person who yields to Him.

In Lucifer's attempt at exaltation, he was out of grace, out of favour and out of order. It was impossible for him to have prospered. This is the beauty of the work of the Almighty God, who wills that all heaven and earth may know His supremacy and the boundlessness of His power and wisdom. From the first line of the passage above in Isaiah, before even going into the details of Lucifer's attempt, the Word tells us of his end. Because this is the end of all rebellion (rebellious people). Oh! How art thou fallen..., how art thou cut down to the ground!

Rebellion is an act or show of defiance towards an established authority or convention (New English dictionary). The intriguing idea is that these rebellions start discreetly, it started in Lucifer's heart. It starts in our heart, away from the views of others, hidden in a place that is not much frequented, it is usually not expressed openly, but sooner or later it bears fruits and fruits are visible evidence. The writing of this book is not actually about Lucifer's rebellion. It is about my rebellion, your rebellion, our rebellion, as we tend to try to usurp God's authority from time to time in our lives. I implore you to search yourself deeply, to visit these secluded places in our minds and hearts to identify these rebellions before they take root and bear fruit.

One Chance

The Lesser thing should not the greater hide
For light and lust are deadly enemies
Shame folded up in concealing night
O, that prone lust should stain so pure a bed
O Iniquity, to drown so precious a soul

Spots which tears nor weeping could cleanse
Blemishes, washed by His blood alone
No need to weep eternally
For His blood doth ever cleanse
Should guilt my master be?
But peace shall rule my heart

We our lives had dearly lost
Yet we, gloriously hath gained it
The dog to its vomit, I won't
Though the past beckons, I must forget
To press for the mark I will

Man hast but one life, soul, spirit
Once a child, adolescent and adult
As a tree, doth he always grow
It needs always bear fruit
Re-incarnation is not possible
No second life

All I have, is one voice
By which I'll be heard
One life by which I'll be known
One moments, in which a difference is made
One chance to shine

The deaf must hear His voice
My light must shine to the blind
With my only life, previously will I
Take the chance to be
Holy just as God is holy

A puppy becomes a dog, and can't return
In one decision, I became God's child
The butterfly to its cocoon, once entered
I'm out of my cave and will not return
Cause all I need is one chance,
To walk into destiny!

Rebellion is a Cancer

In the human, the process of growth and differentiation which occurs is controlled by genes, systemic hormones, position within the fetus (developing baby), local growth factors and matrix proteins. Differentiation is the process whereby a cell develops a specialized function which was not present in its parent cell. It is an important step in the process by which limbs and organs are formed, known as morphogenesis. The maintenance of differentiated state is dependent upon the persistence of some of these factors; this process can be disturbed by environmental factors, such as cancer causing factors called teratogens.

The body of Christ (the church) is also under a process of growth, the process of becoming the bride of Christ. In becoming the chosen bride, it has differentiated members, who have been assigned a unique role within the body. In the case of the church, its morphogenesis is governed and shaped by the Holy Spirit and the Word of God.

> *"And we all, who with unveiled faces contemplate[a] the Lord's glory, are being transformed into his image with ever-increasing glory, which comes from the Lord, who is the Spirit".*
>
> *(2 Corinthians Ch.3 vv18)*

The identity of the body of Christ is based on the spiritual gene we carry. We are generated naturally from the first man Adam. However we have been regenerated through the blood of Christ Jesus, by our faith in Him. In other words we have been re-gened, given a new spiritual DNA, so that we can reproduce and grow after the author of this DNA under the influence of a Master switch, the Holy Spirit.

Cancer is characterized by abnormal growth of cells and abnormal behaviour of cells, which with time lead to the destruction of the surrounding tissue and can lead to the death of the person. The process of a cell becoming cancerous often is preceded by a cell in the body becoming dysplasic. Dysplasia is characterized by increased cell growth over what is normal, usually initiated by a chronic physical or chemical injury. It may be reversible in the early stages, but when allowed to persists it leads to the formation of a neoplastic (cancerous) state.

We can view this on many levels, on the level of the

individual for one. Where for instance our mind and thought life can suffer injury when we allow it to be exposed to a substance that injures it. It then undergoes a change (dysplasia) which is initially reversible, if the maligning offender is removed. This offender could be exposure to pornography, listening a lot to ungodly music, keeping bad company. If the offender is not addressed our mind/thoughts start to become changed for the worse in a permanent way. Even then it still can be treated, but not only by removing the offender, further appropriate treatment usually involves removing the tumour that is destroying the body. Because at this stage, the change persists even after the initiating stimulus has been withdrawn.

The word 'neoplasia' itself actually means new growth, the neoplasm is an abnormal tissue mass, the excessive growth of which is uncoordinated with that of normal tissues, and which persists after the removal of the neoplasm (tumour) inducing stimulus.

When we look at it this way, we can relate it to our personal life. Such is the nature of rebellion, it can cause a part of ourselves to behave in a way that is abnormal and uncoordinated with our new nature. Rebellion within the church, within our government causes individuals or groups of individuals to behave in ways which are abnormal and uncoordinated with the rest of the organism, whether it be the Church of God, or the government of a country.

As the rebellion (cancer) spreads, it causes chaos, destruction and eventually death. It is noteworthy, that the uncontrolled growth and often disordered differentiation of cancers, is always excessive and purposeless. This teaches me that rebellion can breed in minds that have lost or failed to understand God's purpose for them. The formation of neoplasms (tumours), is possible because the cell/s involved are wrested away from their normal control mechanisms. So those who are in rebellion and entertain rebellion, are being wrestled away from the control of the Holy Spirit.

CHAPTER 4

The Lying Heart

"The heart is deceitful above all things and beyond cure. Who can understand it?"

(Jeremiah Ch.17 vv9)

Our intentions can seem good, they usually sound good and we get the commendation of people because of our good intentions. Many times I have had good intentions towards people but the outcome of my actions have been less than good. We can identify with this; it has been on our hearts/minds to respond to the needs of those that are in our circle. We then find that instead of blessing them without looking for a reward, we can use them and even abuse them. In our relationships we can use each other and abuse each other, because each party is mostly concerned about meeting their own needs. The problem is not that they don't think of the other person, but the issue is what they want is above what is needful for the other person.

Imagine a man who has feelings for a woman, or it could be vice versa. The man declares his feelings and the two embark on a relationship for different reasons. Let's say this man is comfortable financially. The man starts dating the woman because he loves her, while the woman enters the relationship because of what she can gain from being in a relationship with him. Despite the fact she knows, she does not have an iota of feeling towards the man. Their relationship can continue with both parties playing a role, the man being led on, as he starts to believe the woman is falling in love with him.

Then a day comes when the woman has gained what she needs, or maybe her wants can no longer be satisfied, or let us say she has found someone else who she thinks can meet her needs. She ends the relationship at this point, betraying the man's heart and confidence, and inadvertently bringing an end to the illusion that he had lived. Who is this woman? I'm not talking about you or am I? Now let's say the man represents Christ, am I talking about you? This is a description of a possible real life scenario between two people. Our Christian lives, and relationship with God can resemble this scenario. Have we entered into God's covenant for our own selfish reasons?

Looking back I've had instances when my aunts have asked me to babysit while I was preparing for exams or had a lot of academic work to do. Asking me to babysit wasn't wrong, but in retrospect it wasn't the best for me, it happened because they learnt I didn't say no to requests. Thank God I'm a bit wiser now. Looking at Numbers chapter 22, we see that Balaam knows the will of God, and initially appears to do what God wants. It even feels like he was enthusiastic about what the Spirit was revealing regarding God's mind concerning Israel; but in later scriptures we learn that he found a way to get what he wanted despite what God said. He met with Balac and taught him to cast a stumbling block before the Israelites so that they might fall in battle (Revelations Ch2 vv14).

> *Nevertheless, I have a few things against you: there are some among you who hold to the teaching of Balaam, who taught Balak to entice the Israelites to sin so that they ate food sacrificed to idols and committed sexual immorality."*
>
> *(Revelations Ch2 vv14)*

In our lives we get what we want despite what God says. We find a way to have what we desire despite what we confess. We can look at certain spheres of our life. If we take a look at relationships, many Christians might confess that they would remain virgins till they get married, but in their relationships they have a distinction between petting and sex. The scripture says "flee youthful lust". Another example is driving uninsured or without a licence, we can give various reasons for the things we do, but the bible says an unjust weight is an abomination before the Lord.

God knows our hearts; he knows when the confession of our lips is contrary to the true desires of our hearts. With our minds we can affirm that the way of the Lord is perfect, just and good. We know this in our hearts; however we do not naturally want the things that God desires. It is my prayer that our hearts will be restored to the place where we are sold out for God, where 'I' humbles itself and is bent that the world may see 'Christ' in you. We need an introspective look into our hearts, to examine and identify the areas which we have deemed above the will and teachings of Christ. I have heard many

Christians say I know the bible says the only case for divorce is infidelity, but why would you continue in a marriage you are not enjoying, where there is no love, where there is no peace, where there is no joy. The truth is Christ came to be the love, peace, joy, truth and much more in the marriage. Here we see many like Balaam exhibiting the symptom of truce breaking; it is the symptom of a dishonest heart, of a heart that is not totally yielded to God. It is evidence of selfishness.

There is no problem with our wants except, that we can make it sovereign over what is good/ what God wants. As such we tend to find ways to have our way despite what God wants and says.

> "Woe to them! They have taken the way of Cain: they have rushed for profit into Balaam's error; they have been destroyed in Korah's rebellion."
>
> (Jude Ch.1 vv11)

The action that ensues in spite of our numerous intentions can usually be symptomatic of what our hearts are after, whether it is the pride of life, or a heart that is drawn away by greed and other lusts. The story of Balaam depicts how a person can find a way to do what he/she wants despite what God said.

There have been times in my life when though I knew the heart of God regarding a matter, I still went on and found a way to do what I wanted to do. With my mouth my confession was that I only want to do what is in God's will, but in my heart I felt drawn away by my own lust. In some of these circumstances I usually come to a compromise, trying to keep myself from going against God's will but attempting to enjoy what I desire at the same time. What I discovered in these situations was that I often up ended up out of position.

The picture that comes to my mind of being out of position was a time when I woke up early to check whether my car had been damaged. The night before I had been up late and had been driving a lot. I was very tired from driving and after dropping a friend home, I got home at about 2 am in the morning. When I parked on the roadside I felt the car wasn't straight and that it was sticking out a bit unto the road, but the rational in my mind was that I would be using it in the morning anyway, so it should be ok. To cut the story short, as I arrived to my car in the morning, the side mirror facing the roadside had been knocked off.

I was annoyed, but in that I learnt a lesson. During daylight it was quite clear to me that my car was out of position, and I realized that when you are out of position, there is a tendency for you to suffer loss. I'm still learning this lesson in my life. In all the areas in which I could be out of position, like spending more than I earn, I shouldn't then be surprised that times become hard later on in the month, and yet I can spend time on my knees asking God to provide.

In contrast to me being out of position, I have a Christian brother. He worked for seven years in a fast-food restaurant in Nigeria. His wages was appalling and he was barely able to support his family, despite having a degree. Of course he was dissatisfied with his situation, but he trusted in God. One day he was visited by a man in the restaurant where he was manager; this man was looking for someone to oversee a chain of restaurants in Abuja (Nigeria), which was currently failing due to poor management. After several meetings with the man and interviews the man offered him the job, and stated that the reason why he hired him was because of his work experience in the fast food industry. Now he is earning more than ten times what he was being paid before, his new accommodation is paid for by the company and he has a company car. When he related this story to me as we sat in the parlour of his new apartment, I was comforted in that as long as we remain in the position God has placed us in, he makes our experiences relevant to our breakthrough.

An outward exhibition of compromise to God's truth is a symptom of a heart that is in rebellion. Rebellion is not always overt, not necessarily palpable, obvious or shown. At times the carrier of that rebellion might be unaware or in denial of the rebellion that is in his or her own heart. Many times I've been in acquainted with some people and my heart was not with them, and I didn't enjoy their company or myself. I hope I'm not the only one that has had this experience; the point I'm making is that because someone sits and agrees with you outwardly doesn't mean that they are with you. Because someone says I do, doesn't necessarily mean they've pledged their hearts and bodies to you. These are hard truths in our daily lives, so now suppose that they are also true regarding our walk with God.

I've heard a friend of mine say 'If God is not Lord of all

your life; He is not Lord of anything'. My intent is not to stir up shame, guilt or condemnation, but to stir up a heart of honesty. To bring us to a place where we are honest with ourselves regarding the small or major areas in our lives in which we are secretly rebellious, these areas can be exhibited by the symptom of compromise, by us failing to admit our weaknesses. The lesson in this passage is that compromise with God's truth causes us to be out of position, and when we are out of position; there is a risk of loss or many losses.

The professional golfer, greatest PGA player of all time announced in December 11, 2009 that he was taking leave from golfing following revelations about his many infidelities, these revelations coming after his wife was seen with a baseball bat trying to get to him in the car he had just crashed. Tiger Woods lost his reputation, his wife, money and much more because of compromise with his weakness. Rebecca Brooks, former News of the World editor, lost her job over the phone hacking scandal of 2011, despite her initial claims that she knew nothing about it.

Many footballers, sportsmen and entertainers have lost money, sponsorship, relationships due to compromise with infidelity, participating in bribery, cheating to name a few. Their stories remind us that it is not as simple as I first put it; many times we will be under incredible pressure to compromise with the truth and with what is right. Looking at their ends, we know we can only expect significant loss.

Dare I say the price to pay for compromise is too high, so

it is worth confronting the secret rebellions in our hearts, before they become symptomatic in our attitudes, marriages, work place, and before they become public knowledge in the world at large? I would debate that the wrongs that we do are mostly symptomatic of the rebellion that lies in our hearts. The important note in this section is that the idea of the hidden rebellion applies to all relationships. From the wife disrespecting her husband to the child playing truant from school.

God's mercy helps us to see that we've lived a lie. It protects us, it doesn't allow our losses due to compromise to be calamitous, and His grace is able to help us to stand in His truth.

> *"He has not dealt with us after our sins nor rewarded us according to our iniquities. For as the heavens are high above the earth, so great are His mercy and loving-kindness toward those who reverently and worshipfully fear Him"*
> *(Psalm Ch.103 vv10 – 11 (amplified bible).*

Covenant breaking

One of the main symptoms of a lying heart is truce breaking; they have the characteristics of breaking agreements, or in the place of peace they sow discord without reason. Like some of the examples above, we can cite acts of infidelity, divorce, cheating your opponents. Such individuals do not realize that faithfulness is important and covenants carry weight. Especially covenants ordained by God such as marriage.

In the book of Ezekiel, chapter 17. God tells a parable of an eagle who took one of the highest branches of the cedars of Lebanon and planted it in good soil so that it grew to become a young vine, however in time it stretched its roots to another eagle. Then the Lord makes this statement

"⁸ It had been planted in good soil by abundant water so that it would produce branches, bear fruit and become a splendid vine."

⁹ 'Say to them, "This is what the Sovereign LORD says: will it thrive? Will it not be uprooted and stripped of its fruit so that it withers? All its new growth will wither. It will not take a strong arm or many people to pull it up by the roots".

There is an important covenant that we have broken; we have broken our covenant with God.

God holds covenants in high esteem; He has been faithful to His word and to His promises to us. We have been unfaithful, although God had planted us in a good soil by great waters that we should bring forth branches and bear fruit. Although he provides for us, and satisfies us with his goodness, we have stretched our roots and branches to other gods; we have given His praise and honour unto another. We've thanked another god for what the Almighty provided. We've served another with the strength and talent that the Lord Almighty had given us.

Yet in all this we are not forsaken.

"²⁵ This is what the LORD says: "If I have not made my covenant with day and night and established the laws of heaven and earth, ²⁶ then I will reject the descendants of Jacob and David my servant and will not choose one of his sons to rule over the descendants of Abraham, Isaac and Jacob. For I will restore their fortunes[e] and have compassion on them."

(Jeremiah Ch.33 vv25 – 26)

This is how unchangeable God's faithfulness and mercy towards us is. Just as there is day and night without fail, He will not cast us off.

"without natural affection, trucebreakers, false accusers, incontinent, fierce, despisers of those that are good." (I Timothy Ch3 vv3) Verse one of this chapter begins with, ' this know also, that in the last days...')

Have we become men and women that have no regard for that which is good, that do not honour an agreement, and do not abide by the terms of contract. In our world when leaders are trying to effect change from a global perspective, they usually tend to get the leaders of other nations in the world to sign a treaty (contract) that is binding. What word do we live in when a man's word is no longer his bond, and basically everyone's promise is a lie.

I will not in this instance bother to discuss on the possible and serious consequences from having a culture of truce-breaking and disrespect of contracts. What I do intend to demonstrate is just how serious a problem it is, why it is rebellion and why God finds it serious. Let us now return to Ezekiel 17, where I believe God reminds the people of Israel what has happened to their princes and kings who went back from following God's word. In other words, they broke God's treaty; they broke truce so that there was enmity between them and God.

This is very fitting, as a truce is established as terms of keeping the peace. From a Christian perspective we enter into a treaty with God, or we enter into God's peace and rest when we give our lives to Jesus, so that the enmity of God that was against us as a consequence of our sins is overturned and rather we are able to enjoy God and revel in His glory.

> *"Say now to the rebellious house, know ye not what these things mean? Tell them, behold, the king of Babylon is come to Jerusalem, and hath taken the king thereof, and the princes thereof, and led them with him to Babylon: And hath taken of the king's seed, and made a covenant with him, and hath taken an oath of him; he hath also taken the mighty of the land. That the kingdom might be base, that it might not lift itself up, but that by keeping of his covenant it might stand. But he rebelled against him in sending his ambassadors into Egypt, that they might give him horses and much people. Shall he prosper? Shall he escape that doeth such things? Or shall he break the covenant and be delivered? As I live, saith the Lord God, surely in the place where the king dwelleth that made him king, whose oath he despised, and whose covenant he break,*

even with him in the midst of Babylon he shall die."

(Ezekiel Ch17 vv12 – 16)

Shall we break God's covenants and expect to succeed?

"Therefore thus saith the Lord God; As I live, surely mine oath that he hath despised, and my covenant that he hath broken, even it will I recompense upon his own head." *(Vs 19)*

There is no escape if we break God's covenant, because He is the God that lives forevermore, and was and is to come. And He has sworn by Himself, saying as I live. With what trembling and fear would we hold unto His covenants, seeing He lives forevermore!

CHAPTER 5

A Show of Defiance

In our world today a show of defiance is prevalent: Students rioting, burning cars and buildings, children coming home late despite their parents' instructions. Committing crimes despite laws that prohibit such crimes such as fraud, rape, murder and many more. What about the show of defiance that comes from the people that are worshipped in the media? We can talk for example about a former talk show presenter that says there is more than one way to God, and the notion that there can only be one way to God is untrue.

> *"For if by one man's offence death reigned by one: much more they which receive abundance of grace and of the gift of righteousness shall reign in life by one, Jesus Christ. Therefore, as by the offence of one judgement came upon all men to condemnation, even so by the righteousness of one the free gift came upon all men unto justification of life. For as by one man's disobedience many were made sinners, so by the obedience of one shall many be made righteous."*
>
> *(Rom Ch.5 vv17 – 19)*

Or the show of defiance by musicians who worship and

magnify evil, they glorify demons in their lyrics, and through their lyrical melody perpetuate a message of disorder, hate, envy, lust. Saying in their songs, that these things are acceptable and should be the normal way of life. It seems to me that in this time that there is a spirit of rebellion gripping the hearts of men and women in our generation, and I feel we are and will continue to deal with its symptoms in these times. So, not only is our heart naturally rebellious against God's order, but we are also surrounded with such influence, that encourages rebellion.

In this age there is an increasing awareness of secret organisations like the 'Illuminati' and 'Free masons'. They propagate a contrary message that the devil is light and was unjustly thrown from heaven, and they have been charged with the task of completing his work through various means which they deploy. Some of their famous symbols include the unfinished pyramid, and the all Seeing Eye, which represent a ridiculous claim that you become illuminated by accepting the authority of the devil. The truth is that there are many other secret organizations that promote ideas that are contrary to the truth. Throughout history they have always operated in secrecy, and have had members who were powerful and well known in society.

The simple truth of these secret organizations is that they practice witchcraft which many people do not know about. They tamper with things that are forbidden. They engage in wicked ceremonies which include activities such as sexual orgies, these can range from heterosexual sex to homosexual sex, even the sexual abuse of children. They also engage in sacrifices to demons, these can be animal or human sacrifices. These things they endeavour to keep from the public eye, on the other hand through the people of influence, wealth and power they have, they propagate subtle devilish messages which propagate rebellion against the order of God.

I would be so bold as to say that the influence of these organizations is responsible for some ideas becoming more easily accepted, in recent times. Such as casual sex in our society, homosexuality, atheism, other forms of spiritualism that do not look to the one true God. Like I've already mentioned they can propagate some of these messages through music, i.e. rock music and other forms of music. If we were to examine some of the lyrics that were being sung, we would be more convinced. We can have a famous artist singing lines like 'I pray to a God that I don't believe in'. And we are surprised when there is an increasing number of children born to Christian families that declare they don't believe in God, we are surprised when our children graduate out of the State educational system with an atheistic world view.

Today we are faced with a rising tide of militant secularism. Firstly as I've mentioned, there has been an increase in those who have an atheistic view. Secondly there is an increase, especially among the rich and famous, in the number of those turning to alternate religions and forms of spirituality. These can include techniques such as yoga which they claim bring them to a place of spiritual oneness and peace. Then there is the turning away of many to other mainstream religions like Islam or Hinduism.

Statistically there has been a fall in the number of people

that identify themselves as Christians today, compared to ten years ago. Regular weekly church attendance has fallen since the middle of the twentieth century. Most worrying of these reasons I have mentioned here, is the secularism that is rising among those that call themselves Christians. Today the percentage of people who identify themselves as Christians is 54%, compared with 72% in 2001 (Ipsos Mori Poll by the Richard Dawkin Foundation). According to a recent academic study non-religious parents are effective at transferring their non-religious beliefs, while a family of two religious parents only have a 50% chance of transferring their religious belief to their children; this is further reduced when only one parent has a religious belief.

In the United Kingdom today, many who call themselves Christians do not practice Christianity; they do not all attend church, some do not read their bibles, some to not adhere to Christian values and teachings. Many welcome the secular notion proposed in many ways by the society we live in.

These shows of defiance are usually led by famous people or a majority. This is one of the important aspects of rebellion. In Numbers 16, we can see an example of a show of defiance against the Almighty God.

"Now Korah, the son of Izhar, the son of Kohath, the son of Levi and Dathan and Abram, the sons of Eliab, and On, the son of Peleth, sons of Reuben, took men; and they rose up before Moses, with certain of the children of Israel, two hundred and fifty princes of the assembly, famous in the

congregation, men of renown: And they gathered themselves together against Moses and against Aaron, and said unto them, ye take too much upon you, seeing all the congregation are holy, every one of them, and the Lord is among them: wherefore then lift ye up yourselves above the congregation of the Lord?"

(Numbers Ch.16 vv1-3)

People that lead rebellion are often supported by a majority, they take solace and comfort in the opinion and support of others, but for the person who is willing to walk uprightly; his comfort and support is in the Lord. Rebellion is not effective without the ability of those who perpetuate it to rally support for their rebellious ideas. Therefore they tend to be persuasive people, people of influence, renowned men and women. If they were not, no one would give heed to their ridiculous propaganda.

Walking in rebellion can be due to a failure to acknowledge that all authority is given by God. Leaders of rebellion tend to be active in persuading and recruiting people to join their cause. The Bible says;

"Let every soul be subject unto the higher powers. For there is no power but of God: the powers that be are ordained of God. Whosoever therefore resisteth the power, resisteth the ordinance of God: and they that resist shall receive to themselves damnation."

(Romans Ch.13 vv1-2)

Attributes of the secret rebellion are an unchanging attitude, repeating offences despite being aware of one's errors, challenging authority usually with no knowledge or incomplete knowledge. The heart of rebellion says I know better, and as such I should have the final say over my life, either in one aspect or in all aspects. In contrast to this a heart of submission and obedience says 'God knows better', so making Him qualified to make the decisions for my life, and making Him worthy of my trust.

> *"Seemeth it but a small thing unto you, that the God of Israel hath separated you from the congregation of Israel, to bring you near to himself to do the service of the tabernacle of the Lord, and to stand before the congregation to minister unto them? And he hath brought thee near to Him, and all thy brethren the sons of Levi with thee: and seek ye the priesthood also? For which cause both thou and all thy company are gathered together against the Lord: and what is Aaron that ye murmur against him?"*
>
> *(Numbers Ch16 vv9 – 11)*

Here we see Moses laying bare what was really in the heart of the sons of Korah. Looking at their request in the early verses we could actually agree with them that they have a point. We could think that they had a genuine concern and reason to bring this charge against Moses and Aaron. We see this in our democratic world today, where everyone has a voice, which is not a problem. Except when this freedom of speech and expression is truly just rebellion, and people not being satisfied with the positions they have and have been given.

We are presented by the Western media with the idea of

democracy being the best form of government. I don't agree with that, neither do I think it's communism, nor a dictarian style, nor am I recommending the idea of a republic. I don't know so much about politics, but I do know the perfect form of government is a theocracy, where God is the ruler. We were created for God's glory and His worship; we see this idea portrayed clearly in the first book of Samuel. Samuel was the last of the judges before Israel had a King, he was also a prophet.

In the first book of Samuel we are told that then the people of Israel asked for a king over them so that they could be like the nations that are surrounding them. This displeased Samuel, but then God spoke to him and reminded him they have not rejected you but have rejected me. Are there echoes in today's World, when we reject the sovereign rule of God for a human King, for the ideas that flow from the minds of Prime ministers, Presidents, Queens and the House of Lords? I'm not saying these forms of governments are evil, but that the fact that we have these rulers and when these rulers have placed their opinions above God's word is flawed in the first instance.

"Then all the elders of Israel gathered themselves together, and came to Samuel unto Ramah. And said unto him, Behold, thou art old, and thy sons walk not in thy ways: now make us a king to judge us like all the nations. But the thing displeased Samuel, when they said, give us a king to judge us. And Samuel prayed unto the Lord. And the Lord said unto Samuel. Hearken unto the voice of the people in all that they say unto thee, for they have

not rejected thee, but they have rejected me, that I
should not reign over them."

(1 Samuel Ch.8 vv4 – 7)

After they had brought this idea forward and God had answered Samuel, God also spoke to them about the consequences of them having a human king.

"And he said, this will be the manner of the king
that shall reign over you: He will take your sons,
and appoint them for himself, for his chariots, and to
be his horsemen; and some shall run before his
chariots. And he will appoint him captains over
thousands, and captains over fifties; and will set
them to ear (sow) his ground, and to reap his harvest,
and to make his instruments of war, and instruments
of his chariots. And he will take your daughters to
be confectionaries, and to be cooks, and to be bakers.
And he will take your fields, and your vineyards,
and your olive yards, even the best of them and give
them to his servants. And he will take the tenth of
your seed, and of your vineyards, and give to his
officers, and to his servants. And ye shall cry out in
that day because of your king which ye shall have
chosen you; and the Lord will not hear you in that
day. Nevertheless the people refused to obey the
voice of Samuel, and they said, nay: but we will
have a king over us: That we also may be like all the
nations; and that our king may judge us, and go out
before us, and fight our battles".

(Verses 11 – 20)

Reading this segment of scripture brings a smile to my

face, it makes me wonder if our politicians and rulers have read this part. In truth that's why we've got to pay taxes, it's actually wrong not to pay your tax. The part I find interesting is of the things the king will make you do and take from you. We can learn that as a result of having 'human rulership' over us we actually rightfully lose some personal choice, like for example the fact that in times of need as during the world wars, able young men had to enlist to fight for their country. During the world wars there came a time when it was almost not optional unless you were excused by your country. The popular phrase was that 'your country had need of you!'

Let me re-iterate I'm not condemning human rulership, but I'm saying it's in rebellion to God when it is not subject to God's authority. I'm also trying to illustrate a point, that 'we are indeed servants to whosoever we obey'. The fact that we lose personal choice on some issues like paying taxes, in times of need enlisting in the army, more importantly obeying the law of the land, is not a matter of your choice, but an illustration of your role as a servant to your nation. It is an understanding that people who think otherwise need to reach. We are all under authority to one degree or another. In the home, in our schools, in our place of work, in the nations where we live and of which we are citizens. To reject the authority over you is an act of rebellion.

The other point I'm getting at is; that we cannot afford to be a servant/slave to the devil and its demons. More correctly as it is put in the letter to the Galatians, we cannot continue to be servants to the desires of the flesh. For rebellion has a captivity, the devil doesn't want servants, his plots are so evil he makes slaves. He doesn't ask for your opinion, he will if you allow him to; enslave you against your will, without your knowledge or prior consent, and with your consent if you are willing. He doesn't tell you the consequences of serving him, but rather will feed you lies. At this we shouldn't be surprised because he was a liar and a murderer from the beginning.

One of the origins of rebellion is a heart of discontent, not being satisfied with the purpose that you've been given and wanting to take a higher position simply because you're envious of it. The reason we might present on the surface might seem genuine, but the heart of it is wicked. When people take part in rebellion, at times they are right in what they are saying and in their claims, but they are wrong in protocol, principle and are out of order. Looking back at the story of Jonah earlier on in the book, his reasons seemed good, but he achieved them out of divine order. His ending might have been negative, but in life he truly might have succeeded; but he still started out of order.

Now in our day we see many uprising in the world, especially in the Arab world of late in 2011, which has been termed 'the Arab Spring'. What we see is a symptom of the heart of the people, who have decided that their leaders are not qualified to lead them; in Libya, Tunisia, Morocco, Syria, Togo and all the other countries, where the people have risen against their government. This show of defiance was a cry of the people saying to their leaders, you are not qualified to lead us, for we know better and we deserve better than you. In some cases the masses are saying we can do better than you've done thus far.

I wouldn't even proceed to dictate on whether these uprisings were right or wrong. God knows all things, what I intend to draw from these stories are the reflections that echoes in our hearts. All authority is given of God; these uprisings are acts of rebellion, an attempt to bring about a revolution in the order of their society. God is sovereign and He uses a myriad of means to raise up rulers and to bring down rulers, this principle can be seen in the vision of Daniel concerning King Nebuchadnezzar. However, when we as Christian people, revolt against leaders that God has placed over us we are not only in rebellion against such leaders but in rebellion against God. As a result of the Arab spring, some leaders have been deposed, killed in the case of Gaddafi, but we serve a God who is incapable of death.

> *"For which cause both thou and all thy company are gathered together against the Lord: And what is Aaron, that ye murmur against him?"*
>
> *(Numbers Ch.16vv 11)*

Rebellion against God shows a lack of understanding and knowledge about the supremacy of God in the Universe, in the world, in government, in schools, in the family, in the individual life. Take for instance our educational system, at some point in history it has been made to propagate a vigorous rebellion against God in the form of the theory of evolution. We are familiar with its teaching, which is falsely called science, as it doesn't obey the laws of empirical science. It was not always so from the beginning. The word tells us that in the beginning God created the heavens and the earth, and we know that there was no one with God in the beginning, neither was there anyone that instructed or advised Him.

Those who propagate the message of evolution, deny the ordinances of God claiming that the earth was formed, over billions of years. In the science books our children study at school, they groom them with the story, that millions of years ago there were dinosaurs that walked the earth and they are now all extinct. They say that all organic beings are formed from a reaction of chemicals; there is also the ridiculous hypothesis of the big bang. All these claims they have made, are contrawise to the truth of God, unable to demonstrate in a reproducible way any of these theories as plausible, with incomplete and manipulated evidence as their rock of truth.

They claim the fossil record is one of the proofs of evolution, but the fact that the order of the fossil record does not scientifically match up with the order that evolution proposes. Yet they have successfully caused many to buy into the lie, that their grandfather was a chimpanzee, and their great-great-grandfather was a fish (i.e. they have evolved from chimpanzees, and the fish is higher up the evolutionary hierarchy). Let us ask ourselves this question, 'is this how ridiculous our rebellions are?' It should be no surprise as those in rebellion exchange the truth of God for a lie.

Richard Dawkins, a renowned atheist, in a news interview claimed people like him were too intelligent to believe in an imaginary friend, this was in response to Baronness Warsi's warning in February 2012: that 'British society is under threat from the rising tide of "militant secularisation" reminiscent of "totalitarian regimes". Of note Baronness Warsi, is a minister with no religious affiliations. Richard Dawkins went on to emphasize that it is a bit ridiculous to expect society to be more united and people to live better lives by believing in an imaginary friend.

The educational authority and government will not teach the truth. The theory of evolution cannot explain the fossil record; neither does it give an account or any similitude of the truth of our origins. We should in truth be having creationism taught in school, that the world was created in six literal days as in the account of Genesis chapter one, and that the fossil record can be adequately explained by such a cataclysmic event such as the Genesis flood. I would not attempt to appear as an expert on this subject, but one thing I remember firstly. That God is true and let everyman be a liar, there are things we don't fully know and cannot fully understand as we were not there, but we know that the word of God is true. On such a note and on such strength of evidence we can discount every claim made by anyone against the word of God.

> *"Jesus said unto them, if God were your Father, ye would love me: for I proceeded forth and came from God: neither came I of myself, but he sent me. Why do ye not understand my speech? Even because ye cannot hear my word. Ye are of your father the devil, and the lusts of your father ye will do. He was a murderer from the beginning, and abode not in the truth, because there is no truth in him. When he speaketh a lie, he speaketh of his own: for he is a liar, and the father of it".*
>
> *(John Ch8 vv42 -44)*

We see this same pattern in the rebellion of Dathan

and Korah *"Is it a small thing that thou hast brought us up out of a land that floweth with milk and honey, to kill us in the wilderness, except thou make thyself altogether a prince over us? Moreover thou hast not brought us into a land that floweth with milk and honey, or given us inheritance of fields and vineyards: wilt thou put out the eyes of these men? We will not come up".*

(Numbers 16. Verses 13-14)

What Dathan and his company said was the direct opposite of what God had told them. They called Egypt a land flowing with milk and honey, and claimed that they were brought from such a land to be killed in the wilderness. When God had delivered the people of Israel from the house of bondage (Egypt) He was taking them (transitioning them) to the Promised Land (a land flowing with milk and honey).

Manifestations of the secret rebellion in our world

Young people staying out late at night, when their parents/guardians have told them to come home early

Disrespect towards parents
Open disrespect and mocking of elders and authoritative figures i.e. cussing your teacher at school, challenging the church eldership, vandalism of government property, gossiping about your boss

Rebellion basically says, we don't have to do what you said because you said so, but we do what we think is right (because we know better). The reality of these words are 'we don't have to do what God said because He said so, but we do what we think is right – because we know better'. The secret rebellion comes as a result of not understanding the supremacy of God.

Being in rebellion against God is evidence that you are in service to another god. It could be your belly, it could be religion, and it could be money. Your works show who you serve, we can stop at this point to examine the works of some well known groups like Al qaeda. Let's take 'Boko Haram' for example, a radical terrorist group that is thought to be the Nigerian Al qaeda branch, who are bent on causing the government to impose Muslim sharia law over Nigeria, at least over the Northern parts. A country that is essentially split in half religiously, with 50% of the population being Muslims and the other 50% being Christians.

Boko Haram have been involved in several terror attacks over the last few years in Nigeria, they've bombed the US embassy in Abuja, bombed churches while worshippers were inside and have committed many other sinister attacks against civilians. More recently they are maintaining a tirade of attacks against innocent Christian worshippers. In January 2011 within the space of three days they murdered thirty Christians, on Friday 6th of January the murder of 11 men and one woman, then on the following thursday they killed 17 people while they were mourning the deaths of two others who were killed the day before. These attacks all happened in the city of Mubi (Nigeria).

Boko Haram's attacks have particularly been against

Christians living in the Northern part of Nigeria. They have also attacked police stations. In their acts, they have shown a great disregard for life, for authority and for the citizens of Nigeria. Their acts are evil and their intentions and agenda are mindless. At the height of their campaign, there was a tirade of attacks in January 2012, carried out in the state of Kano (Nigeria), where they killed over 211 people in one day. The Nigerian government drafted in the military to help contain this radical movement.

Thinking of this rebellion against God reminds me of a prophetic verse in the book of Daniel.

> *"And the king shall do according to his will: and he shall exalt himself, and magnify himself above every god, and shall speak marvellous things against the God of gods, and shall prosper till the indignation be accomplished: for that that is determined shall be done. Neither shall he regard the God of his fathers, nor the desire of women, nor regard any god: for he shall magnify himself above all. But in his estate shall he honour the God of forces: and a god whom his fathers knew not shall he honour with gold, and silver, and with precious stones, and pleasant things. Thus shall he do in the most strong -holds with a strange god, whom he shall acknowledge and increase with glory: and he shall cause them to rule over many, and shall divide the land for gain."*
> *(Daniel Ch11 vv36-39)*

It seems like the hearts of many are going a similar way. Once we served gods that were not God, then our fathers turned to serve the living God, and we being mindful of the knowledge of the living God, do we now turn to serve that which is not the true living God?

The manifestation of this rebellion applies to all relationships. There has to be order in relationships, there are boundaries that define every relationship. As I mentioned already, you can be right in detail but wrong in principle and manner. The heart of rebellion lies in self-interest, as such rebellion never takes the problem first to God, but takes comfort and strength in human opinion – this is one of the first signs of rebellion.

Rebellion is also leading people along a way that is not godly, that God has not taught.

> *"Ye shall walk after the Lord your God, and fear him, and keep his commandments, and obey his voice, and ye shall serve him, and cleave unto him. And that prophet, or that dreamer of dreams, shall be put to death; because he hath spoken to turn you away from the Lord your God, which brought you out of the land of Egypt, and redeemed you out of the house of bondage, to thrust thee out of the way which the Lord thy God commanded thee to walk in. So shalt thou put the evil away from the midst of thee. If thy brother the son of thy mother, or thy son, or thy daughter, or the wife of thy bosom, or thy friend, which is as thine own soul, entice thee secretly, saying, Let us go and serve other gods, which thou hast not known, thou, nor thy fathers;"*
> *(Deuteronomy Ch13 vv4-6)*

Therefore watch out for friends and family, do not be

enticed by their rebellion, neither conceal them but rather reveal it.

A rebellious person fails to understand that all authority comes from God, as we can learn from Paul's writings in the book of Romans, regarding the authority of the king, of government, of church leadership and in other places the positions of authority in the family and marriage. If you disrespect someone in authority, you disrespect the person who put them in authority i.e. if wives disrespect their husbands, or husbands fail to love their wives. People in authority have power over you, you wouldn't want them speaking negatively over your life as to bring upon yourself a curse.

From the text in Numbers 16, we are able to see how Moses dealt with Rebellion (verse 4). The authority Moses had, was a spiritual authority, he was able to act in his position of authority versus reacting to the people's provocation. When Moses was challenged, he fell on his face or in other words, turned towards God.

> *"And when Moses heard it, he fell upon his face"*
> *(Numbers Ch16 vv4)*

A question of trust

We have to make decisions all the time. There can be several driving forces for the decisions that we make. In the story at the beginning of this book, the main character Jonah makes his decision based on the potential rewards of making a fortune and a name for himself. What are the

63

motivating or fear factors that drive us to make the decisions for our daily lives? For example, I work away from my family home and I'm usually in the habit of returning home to see the family and to go back to my home church. However in one particular month I didn't often go home because I realized I was broke and didn't want to be in the situation where I had to think about how to survive the rest of the month. In this instance, the fear of not having sufficient wherewithal prevented me from doing what I wanted to do.

> *"Hezekiah trusted in, leaned on, and was confident in the Lord, the God of Israel: so that neither after him nor before him was any one of all the Kings of Judah like him. For he clung and held fast to the Lord and ceased not to follow Him, but kept His commandments, as the Lord commanded Moses. And the Lord was with Hezekiah: he prospered wherever he went. And he rebelled against the King of Assyria and refused to serve him" (Amp bible).*
> *(2 Kings Ch18 vv5 – 7)*

Hezekiah refused to serve the King of Assyria, even though they were mightier than Judah and Judah had been in service to the King of Assyria prior to this. He was only able to prosper in this decision because he trusted in God. His trust in God distinguished him from all the other Kings of Judah that were before him or after him. May God give us this same heart that was in Hezekiah. As followers of God we should be distinguished by our trust in Him.

An attribute of this hidden rebellion is a failure to trust

God in spite of what God has done in the (your) past. A failure to lean on God, to have confidence in the Lord despite of your knowledge of His supremacy and power. Hezekiah decided in his heart not to serve any king but the Lord; he could easily have made excuses, and acted out of fear as I did (as I had created a condition producing a type of fear for myself). However he maintained his belief in God.

> *"And in the wilderness, where thou hast seen how that the Lord thy God bare thee, as a man doth bear his son, in all the way that ye went, until ye came into this place. Yet in this thing ye did not believe the Lord your God, who went in the way before you, to search you out a place to pitch your tents in, in fire by night, to show you by what way ye should go, and in a cloud by day".*
>
> *(Deuteronomy 1 vv31-33)*

God can do mighty acts, and display the splendour of His power and yet we could have an unbelieving heart. Fear and unbelief are the opposite of trust, unbelief breeds fear, without belief in God we have no hope. This life is the end of the journey, our pain; suffering, joy and happiness are meaningless. Hope causes us to have confidence. It is essential to believe and hope for the things that God promises us, living in unbelief comes from a heart of rebellion. A heart that requires God to prove Himself time and time again on our own conditions and because there is wickedness in our hearts will not let us trust God.

We become like the Israelites who worshipped other gods

in the Promised Land, forgetting it was God that led them by the hand through the Red Sea, forgetting that He was the one that led them by a pillar of fire by night and a pillar of cloud by day. Like Jonah forgetting that he prospered in his master's house and thought the prosperity was all down to his talent. His actions are reminiscent of 'Aholah' and 'Aholibah', who played the harlot and forgot it was God that provided for them, and cast Him behind them (Ezekiel Ch.23).

> *"For she has not noticed, understood, or realized that it was I [the Lord God] who gave her the grain and the new wine and the fresh oil, and who lavished upon her silver and gold which they used for Baal and made into his image. Therefore will I return and take back My grain in the time for it and My new wine in the season for it, and will pluck away and recover My wool and My flax which were to cover her [Israel's] nakedness.*
>
> *(Amp bible Hosea Ch2 vv8 -9).*

CHAPTER 6

What Are Our Secret Rebellions?

It is useful at this point to consider: what are our secret rebellions? This might not be the most felicitous question to ponder on, but its eventual impact could be liberating as we would discuss the cure for the hidden rebellion. The whole idea of the secret rebellion is that it is not known to others. It is kept to oneself or only made known to a selected few.

> *"This know also, that in the last days perilous times shall come. For men shall be lovers of their own selves, covetous, boasters, proud, blasphemers, disobedient to parents, unthankful, unholy. Without natural affection, truce-breakers, false accusers, incontinent, fierce, despisers of those that are good. Traitors, heady, high-minded, lovers of pleasures more than lovers of God."*
> *(2 Timothy Ch.3 vv1-4)*

What are your secret rebellions?

Deciding not to pay your tithes, because 'it all goes to the Pastor, besides what are they doing with our money?'

• Wives disrespecting their husbands?

- Husbands not loving their wives

- Unfaithfulness

- A manipulative personality

- Claiming made-up expenses from your employers e.g. if you were an MP

- Illegal hacking of phone calls/voicemail so you can make the news

This list is extensive but not exhaustive. Other manifestations of this secret rebellion in our world include;

- Young people staying out late at night when parents/guardians have told them to be home early

- Disrespect towards parents

- Open disrespect and mocking of elders and authoritative figures i.e. cussing your teacher, challenging the church eldership outside biblical protocol

- Vandalism of government and state property

- Rioting in the streets

- Gossiping about your boss

- Not listening to instructions

- Truce breaking

It is expressed by "the works of the flesh".

> *"Now the works of the flesh are manifest, which are these: Adultery, fornication, uncleanness, lasciviousness, idolatry, witchcraft, hatred, variance, emulations, wrath, strife, seditions, heresies. Envyings, murders, drunkenness, revellings, and such like: of the which I tell you before, as I have also told you in time past, that they which do such things shall not inherit the kingdom of God."*
> *(Galatians Ch.5 vv19 – 21)*

Remember you can be right in what you're saying but wrong in protocol and principle. Our God is a God of order. The rebellious mind lays claim to doing what they think is right because it knows better. John Piper in his book 'The Fear of the Lord' talks about how the fear of God, will return to the church, when divine order is in place. Divine order as in regards to the comprehensible arrangement, or to put more correctly the proper arrangement of the elements of our life and the things of this world, as determined by God. The idea of the church, which is the people of God, is the prophetic unction that would bring the church into conformity with the rules and principles of the kingdom of God. This order emanates from God, and the purpose of the alignment of the church with God's divine order is for wholesome devotion to God, to His worship and for His service.

I'll now talk of King Zedekiah of Israel who wouldn't listen to what God instructed him to do. His actions can be contrasted with that of King Hezekiah of Israel. They both rebelled against very powerful kings by refusing to serve them, however with both very different outcomes.

> *"For Zedekiah king of Judah had shut him up saying,*
> *wherefore dost thou prophesy, and say. Thus saith*
> *the Lord, Behold, I will give this city into the hand*
> *of the king of Babylon, and he shall take it; And*
> *Zedekiah king of Judah shall not escape out of the*
> *hand of the Chaldeans, but shall surely be delivered*
> *into the hand of the king of Babylon, and shall*
> *speak with him mouth to mouth and his eyes shall*
> *behold his eyes: And he shall lead Zedekiah to*
> *Babylon, and there shall he be until I visit him,*
> *saith the Lord, though ye fight with the Chaldeans,*
> *ye shall not prosper?"*
>
> *(Jeremiah Ch.32 vv3-5)*

Zedekiah in the account given of him in the book of Jeremiah continues to show a lack of fear of the Lord; he didn't tremble at the word of the Lord. He knew Jeremiah was a true prophet but he would rather listen to the lying prophets who prophesied lies that the children of Israel were not going to go into captivity than listen to Jeremiah. God continually gave instruction to Zedekiah on what was going to happen to Jerusalem because of its numerous sins. However King Zedekiah would not accept this, because this was not what he wanted, which is totally understandable.

He should have understood that despite the fact that the word of God was contrary to his desires, he shouldn't exchange God's word for lies as he did at times, nor should he have trusted in his own word as he did at other times. The right thing would have been for him to act like

Hezekiah, if he was grieved by the judgement of God, he should have accepted God's word but brought his petition before God. This can be seen in the instance when the word of the Lord came to Hezekiah that he was to die. Hezekiah didn't utter one word to Isaiah, but he turned to the wall and prayed to his God in heaven for mercy. His humility and cry so touched God's heart, that God immediately sent a new word over the life of Hezekiah and changed the decree of death to that of an extended life.

"In those days Hezekiah was sick and near death. And Isaiah the prophet, the son of Amoz, went to him and said to him, Thus says the Lord: set your house in order, for you shall die and not live. Then Hezekiah turned his face toward the wall, and prayed to the Lord, and said, Remember now, O Lord, I pray, how I have walked before You in truth and with a loyal heart, and have done what is good in Your sight. And Hezekiah wept bitterly. And the word of the Lord came to Isaiah, saying, Go and tell Hezekiah, Thus says the Lord, the God of David your father: I have heard your prayer, I have seen your tears: surely I will add to your days fifteen years".

(Isaiah Ch38 vv1-5)

Zedekiah's actions were a symptom of his rebellion. We will see this clearer in the next instant, when king Nebuchadnezzar had come to Jerusalem with his army to fight against Jerusalem. Here God reminds Zedekiah that Jerusalem would be destroyed and he would go into captivity, but that God will spare his life and allow him to die with honour at the right time. Zedekiah listened and walked righteously for a short while, but then again he rebelled against God.

"The word which came unto Jeremiah from the Lord, when Nebuchadnezzar King of Babylon, and all his army, and all the kingdoms of the earth of his dominion, and all the people, fought against Jerusalem, and against all the cities thereof, saying. Thus saith the Lord, the God of Israel, go and speak to Zedekiah King of Judah, and tell him, thus saith the Lord: Behold, I will give this city into the hand of the King of Babylon, and he shall burn it with fire: And thou shalt not escape out of his hand but shalt surely be taken, and delivered into his hand: and thine eyes shall behold the eyes of the king of Babylon, and he shall speak with thee mouth to mouth, and thou shalt go to Babylon. Ye hear the word of the Lord, O Zedekiah king of Judah; thus saith the Lord of thee, thou shalt not die by the sword: But thou shalt die in peace; and with the burnings of thy fathers, the former kings which were before thee, so shall they burn odours for thee; and they will lament thee, saying. Ah lord! For I have pronounced the word, saith the Lord. Then Jeremiah the prophet spake all these words unto Zedekiah king of Judah in Jerusalem."

(Jeremiah Ch.34 vv1-6)

So Zedekiah made a covenant with all the people to proclaim liberty to them, in that they all let their man servants and maid servants go free. This was a command that God had given in the Mosaic laws to the children of

Israel, they were supposed to do this every seventh year. Clearly they had not been doing this. But let's examine verses 10 – 11:

> *"Now when all the princes, and all the people, which had entered into the covenant, heard that everyone should let his manservant, and everyone his maidservant, go free, that none should serve themselves of them anymore, then they obeyed, and let them go. But afterward they turned, and caused the servants and the handmaids, whom they had let go free, to return, and brought them into subjection for servants and handmaids."*

> *(Verse 17) "Therefore thus saith the Lord: Ye have not hearkened unto me, in proclaiming liberty, everyone to his brother, and every man to his neighbour, behold, I proclaim a liberty for you, saith the Lord, to the sword, to the pestilence, and to the famine, and I will make you to be removed into all the kingdoms of the earth".*

In this verse, the people yet again bring judgement upon themselves by turning from the word of God, it teaches us that when we are in difficult times, it's not by doing evil, or trickery/cunning that we can come out of it, but by doing righteousness. When we take hold again upon God's word, we can save ourselves and others from judgement.

In verse 21, there is now a word from God reversing the mercy that God had intended to have on Zedekiah.

> *"And Zedekiah king of Judah and his princes' will I*

give into the hand of their enemies and into the
hand of them that seek their life, and into the hand
of the king of Babylon's army, which are gone up
from you".

Here we see that because of their initial obedience the
king of Babylon and his army left off the siege, as a result
of this the people of Judah and Jerusalem took back their
slaves. It was clear that they didn't love God and their
obedience was partial. When they thought they were out
of danger, they started disobeying the words of God
again! Let us take this moment to ponder, do we turn
away from God's word when all seems like it is going
well and there doesn't seem to be any pressing danger?
Do we fear what men can do to us, and hence feign
obedience?

I am here to inform you, as I have learnt myself; that
obedience is not complete unless it is total obedience,
unless it is unconditional surrender. A surrender that is
not dependent on the economic climate, one that is not
amiable to change based on government policy or popular
opinion, a courage that is willing to remain steadfast in
the face of pressing evil and oppression.

Let's move further into the book of Jeremiah, to chapter
35. At this point the siege had returned to Jerusalem and
Jeremiah had been cast into the dungeon by the princes of
Judah and brought out by Zedekiah.

"Then said Jeremiah unto Zedekiah. Thus saith the
Lord, the God of hosts, the God of Israel: if thou
wilt assuredly go forth unto the king of Babylon's

*princes, then thy soul shall live, and this city shall
not be burned with fire: and thou shalt live, and
thine house. But if thou wilt not go forth to the king
of Babylon's princes, then shall this city be given
into the hand of the Chaldeans, and they shall burn
it with fire, and thou shalt not escape out of their
hand. And Zedekiah the king said unto Jeremiah, I
am afraid of the Jews that are fallen to the
Chaldeans, lest they deliver me into their hand, and
they will mock me. But Jeremiah said, they shall not
deliver thee. Obey, I beseech thee; so it shall be well
unto thee, and thy soul shall live."*

(Jeremiah Ch35 vv17 – 20)

I cannot put it better than Jeremiah did, 'so it will be well
with you and you will live'. God is speaking to us strongly
on the matter of departing from our secret rebellions. He
is promising us life, even when it looks like he's asking us
to commit suicide, like Zedekiah being told to give himself
up to the Chaldeans. God is interested in doing what is
best for us, and He knows best. I can't help but re-iterate
the phrase that John Piper coined saying that 'God is
most glorified, when we are most satisfied in Him'.

Let me conclude this session: eventually the Chaldeans
broke through the wall of Jerusalem, Zedekiah didn't give
himself up but tried to escape through another route.

*"But the Chaldean army pursued after them, and
overtook Zedekiah in the plains of Jericho: and when
they had taken him, they brought him up to
Nebuchadnezzar king of Babylon to Riblah in the
land of Hamath, where he gave judgement upon*

him. Then the king of Babylon slew the sons of
Zedekiah in Riblah before his eyes; also the king of
Babylon slew all thee nobles of Judah. Moreover he
put out Zedekiah's eyes, and bound him with chains,
to carry him to Babylon. And the Chaldeans burned
the king's house, and the houses of the people, with
fire, and brake down the walls of Jerusalem."

(Jeremiah Ch39 vv5 - 8)

Zedekiah ended up losing his sight, and all his family that God promised him He would save if he gave himself up. And he became a captive in Babylon, which was what he was attempting to flee from. We can learn from Hezekiah, from how he sought God in prayer and with many tears. He acknowledged the sovereignty of God and recognised that you cannot fight against someone who is mightier than you.

The Zeal of Obedience

In a sermon I once listened to in church, the visiting pastor gave a testimony of a time in his life when he had to be obedient to God in difficult circumstances. He was supposed to be ministering at another city the next day, but he got a call that his child had died. In the midst of his grief, he could have gone home to be with his wife. But he heard the voice of God telling him that he must go and preach at the place where he had an appointment. He decided to obey the voice of God despite his pain, and that night he was visited by the presence of God in a powerful way. He was overshadowed by the powerful presence of God in the form of a cloud, while he was in his bedroom! How zealous are we in obeying the voice of God that we know?

Most times in our lives our obedience is compromised by fear, opposition, despair, weariness, and even pain. There are times when it is easy to do what is wrong despite knowing what right, can weariness and tiredness be an excuse for disobedience to God's instructions. I am guilty of this, and need to learn to look to the author of our faith. For we see that Christ Jesus was faithful in the midst of opposition, when tempted by fear, or when he was weary he did not accept the dainties that the enemy offered Him, in declaring that man does not live by bread alone. In imitating the captain of our salvation, how do we become zealous to be obedient to our father in heaven, despite the situations and conditions that are against us?

We are afraid because we face uncertainties in the midst of unfamiliar dangers. We face opposition foremost because we have an adversary, secondly because people are selfish and can be ruthless. We are weary because we have fought in our own strength and at times we come to that place where we are all out of energy, when it seems the fight is gone out of us. We are in pain at times, because we have lost so much, many of which were important and precious to us.

Dealing with the mountains and giants

We have established that there are failings in our hearts. I came to a point in my life when I felt that at times my love was not enough. We see situations and circumstances that act as impediments, which prevent us from doing what is right, from thinking right, from having a right heart, from acting right. We can refer to these situations and circumstances as mountains or as giants. I feel it might be helpful to look at them in this way in understanding why and how they prevent us, and in coming to understand what we can do about them.

There are mountains in our lives that face us, we can climb them or refuse to go up them. There are also giants that we meet along the way, who are hasty to try to destroy us or frustrate us as we continue along on our pilgrimage. We suffer reproach when we fail in this. It is useful to ask ourselves the question; what mountains do I face? Could it be:

- An unfinished project – the book you started

- Waiting for an engagement ring

- Waiting for a break in your career

- The business you are currently struggling in

- Financial difficulty - not being able to balance the books

- Great need in the world – the large number of suffering people

- The huge number of unsaved people

- The number of backslidden Christians

- The presence of false doctrines

- The power of false religions

- The task of getting the gospel to the nations

- Finding a wife

- Finding a husband

- Let us also ask ourselves the second question, Which giants are threatening me?

- Debts

- Mortgage

- Unruly children

- Unsaved parents

- Addiction – smoking, drugs, sex, pornography, food

- Laziness

- Immorality – lust, lying, cheating, irresponsibility

- Timidity

- Anger, Bitterness, Hatred, Spitefulness

A mountain is a land mass that projects well above its surroundings. My mountains are the surrounding conditions in my life that seem insurmountable, they are worse than a rough patch (which I'll call a valley), at times they seem insurmountable, they can appear to be always present. We have to deal with these mountains, as we don't live in a Christian bubble, by being Christian we're not immune to the circumstances that face others in the world.

The mountains are situations and circumstances that seem difficult or at times even impossible. They are hindrances to us, they hinder our joy, they hinder our love, they hinder our success, and they can even hinder our destiny.

A giant is someone or something that is abnormally large and powerful. I can define the giants in my life as the forces/things that keep me from becoming the giant God created me to be, the powers that fight to belittle me and stop me from becoming a man of renown. The giants are habits, repetitive sins, yokes, bondages, people, demons that fight against us. They fight us in many ways. They attempt to cause us to compromise our salvation, they move the boundary lines and act to cause us to disqualify ourselves, and they try to kill us, to destroy us. They accuse us before our maker God almighty.

"There were giants in the earth in those days: and also after that, when the sons of God came in unto the daughters of men, and they bare children to them, the same became mighty men which were of old, men of renown."

(Gen 6; 4)

The passage above has been inserted to make us aware

that the presence of giants is not something new, they have always been around. Also we're not the only one facing them but everyone else has to face giants and mountains. The face and nature of the giant may change, but it remains true to its kind, in being a giant.

Despite this, the mountains in our lives can be our stepping stones, so we must climb them. The giants can be our tests for promotions, so we must fight to win, in fighting we can have no excuse for allowing defeat as we confront the giants in our lives. This is a hard truth but is one that is necessary for overcoming and obtaining perpetual victory over the enemy.

We can feel helpless when faced with these mountains; we get the familiar sinking feeling; i.e. Oh! The mortgage is due again and I'll be overdrawn in my account again and the bank will charge me again, whereas on further thought, it is odd because the mortgage is due every month. We could be in a place where it seems that the constant presence of the mountains in our life has us feeling like we are trapped in a vicious cycle.

Do we become filled with doom and gloom, anytime we set foot at work, anytime the bill comes through the post-box? Has it got to the stage where the mountain has made us cry 'how long Lord'. The thing about mountains is that they are so large, that people prefer to go around them rather than climb over them. At times when we come to a mountain it is easier to go back.

Are we tempted to return to old habits, old patterns of doing things because of enormous circumstances that are facing us? Will I return to stealing and living a double life just to put bread on the table, whereas Paul speaks on the contrawise;

> *"Not that I speak in respect of want: for I have learned, in whatsoever state I am, therewith to be content. I know both how to be abased, and I know how to abound: everywhere and in all things I am instructed both to be full and to be hungry, both to abound and to suffer need. I can do all things through Christ which strengtheneth me."*
>
> *(Phillipians Ch.4 vv11 -13)*

In a novel by Jeffrey Archer titled 'Paths of Glory', we see the main character 'George Mallory' who is portrayed as a brave young man that makes it his life ambition to conquer the biggest mountain in the world 'Mount Everest'. Through the story we see how he sees others fail and even die in their bid to conquer their mountains and giants. This doesn't deter him, neither is he deterred even when he is confronted by death on numerous occasions. He had narrow escapes from death, yet his confidence and determination remains. In the version that Jeffrey Archer tells, he conquers his mountain, at the expense of his life.

This novel was based on a true story. Everest is about 29,000 feet high, and at that time in which the story is set, even an aeroplane had not flown at this height. George refers to his driving factor as an obsession. He referred to Everest as 'my lady', and in a letter to his wife while he was away from her on the expedition to conquer everest; he expressed his deep desire 'to conquer this demon' once and for all, so he could return to his life with his wife and family. To him 'Mount Everest' was the mistress he could not leave till he had conquered her, he sought to rid himself of the obsession he had for her.

In the novel, George Mallory makes two attempts at climbing Everest, he fails in the first attempt, but his successful at the second attempt. Despite the great difficulty experienced with the first expedition to conquer Everest, Mr Mallory realised he could not move on in his life till he had reached the peak of Everest.

Sometimes we can feel like the promise is delayed, and so we tire while waiting for God. Doubting if He heard our prayer, doubting if He is on our side, at this stage we can set off to find means of obtaining what we desire. Whether it is the desire to have a soul mate, a desire to get into that career pathway, or start that business. Even Abraham made that mistake, when he thought he could settle for a substitute and gave birth to Ishmeal instead of waiting for Isaac.

The substitute looked good, Ishmeal was Abraham's son, and he could have passed for his heir. Thank God that the promises of God are so sure that despite all; Ishmeal could not pass muster for the promise. I pray that just as jealousy was stirred up in Sarah when she saw Ishmeal (the substitute) mocking the promise (Isaac), Ishmeal had to leave the house. If we have in anyway found a substitute for God's promise, that substitute can no longer be permitted to take the place of the promise or in some instances grow up along with the promise, as Ishmeal did grow up with Isaac for a time.

Is it time to give up that substitute relationship? Is it time to totally give up trying to make ends meet using crooked means, although it feels like God is taking too long? Is it time to start believing in the dream God gave you again, and refuse to settle for what you could obtain in your own might? We can be bold like Moses and refuse to be called the sons of Pharoah and rather choose to suffer with the princes of God (Israel). Even to this day the descendants of Ishmael trouble the descendants of Isaac. Is it possible that whatever you're using as a substitute for God's promise is actively resisting the manifestation of God's promise to you?

Many people in life make it their personal challenge to climb mountains, they call themselves mountaineers. Over the years they have evolved the use of specialized safety and climbing equipment to enable them to scale the tallest mountains in the world, with their reward being their name finding a place in the 'Guinness World book of records' as the world's highest accolade for them.

A phrase that can be used when one has climbed a mountain is that 'I have conquered that mountain'. Well, for some people it might be "I have conquered that hill or that heap or mound". Have you conquered that mountain, have you conquered anything at all? If you are planning to make a start on conquering the mountains in your life, you have to recognize, just as George Mallory did, that there are dangers. There are dangerous precipices on the mountains that can seem impossible to assail, and that can cause your death if you are not careful enough.

Are you frustrated by your lack of conquering ability?

Are we unable to follow in the steps of Alexander the great and say, 'I came, I saw and I conquered!' Or is it rather 'it' came, I saw and I feared!'

If you're in a vicious cycle, are you training intensely like a mountaineer to enable you to scale the mountains that you are suppose to surmount? I do not mean to overwhelm you with such deep soul searching questions, but I'm trying to open your mind to the idea that mountaineers prepare for the expeditions they undertake to climb their mountains.

> *"Now Moses kept the flock of Jethro his father-in-law, the priest of Midian; and he led the flock to the back side of the desert and came to the mountain of God, even to Horeb. And the angel of the LORD appeared unto him in a flame of fire out of the midst of a bush; and he looked and, behold, the bush burned with fire, and the bush was not consumed. And Moses said, "I will now turn aside and see this great sight, why the bush is not burnt."*
> *(Exodus Ch.3 vv1-3)*

There are mountains we have to climb as there is a price at the summit of the mountain, just as for mountaineers. For the angel of the Lord verily appeared unto Moses for the first time; when he came to the mountain of the Lord in Horeb. After that Moses usually went up a mountain to hear from God. Are there mountains where we need to reach the summit to hear from God, for us to have a deeper relationship with God?

(Verse 5) "And he said, draw not nigh hither, put off

thy shoes from off thy feet, for the place whereon thou standest is holy ground."

On Mount Horeb, Moses met the God of the Abrahamic promises.

"So they went up, and searched the land from the wilderness of Zin unto Rehob, as men come to Hamath. And they ascended by the south, and came unto Hebron: where Ahiman, Sheeshai, and Talmai, the children of Anak, were. (Now Hebron was built seven years before Zoan in Egypt.) And they came unto the brook of Eshcol, and cut down from thence a branch with one cluster of grapes,and they bare it between two upon a staff; and they brought of the pomegranates, and of the figs."

(Numbers 13; 21 – 23)

(Verses 27 -28) "And they told him, and said, we came unto the land whither thou sent us, and surely it floweth with milk and honey; and this is the fruit of it. Nevertheless the people be strong that dwell in the land, and the cities are walled, and very great: and moreover we saw the children of Anak there."

(Verses 30 – 33) "And Caleb stilled the people before Moses, and said. Let us go up at once, and possess it; for we are well able too overcome it. But the men that went up with him said, we be not able to go up against the people; for they are stronger than we. And they brought up an evil report of the land which they had searched unto the children of Israel, saying. The land, through which we have gone to search it, is a

*land that eateth up the inhabitants thereof: and all
the people that we saw in it are men of a great stature.
And there we saw the giants, the sons of Anak, which
come of the giants: and we were in our own sight as
grasshoppers, and so we were in their sight."*

The giants in our lives can cause us to be afraid. Just like
the ten spies that Moses sent out to spy the land along
with Joshua and Caleb. These men focussed on how small
they were in comparison to the giants, the sons of Anak.
But Joshua and Caleb focussed on the fact that the land
was a land flowing with milk and honey, they had their
eyes on the price.

Caleb and Joshua's confidence was in that the Lord had
delivered the land unto them, besides they had all
acknowledged that the land was good. Have you come
into a good land and felt unable to possess because of the
giants in it, or the descendants of the giants?

People have conquered mountains, many have killed the
giants that have troubled them. You can defeat the giants
in your life, you can climb most mountains in your life!
Some mountains you would have to speak to them and
there is grace available so that you don't have to climb it.
In these situations we should be reminded that 'it is not
by might, nor by power but by the spirit of the Lord.

We can instil order to situations

We can instil divine order into people's life

Attention to God's word can bring order into our life and

cure the chaos that has long plagued us

We can speak to chains and yokes that they be loosed in the name of Jesus

> *"Who art thou, O great mountain? Before Zerubbabel thou shalt become a plain; and he shall bring forth the headstone thereof with shoutings, crying, 'Grace, grace unto it!"*
>
> *(Zechariah Ch.4 vv7)*

But there are mountains you need to climb; as such we would require divine strategy to climb some mountains. Divine strategies are strategic plans and manoeuvres given by God. Our inability to conquer can also be due to how we see ourselves; we could have a grasshopper mentality. We could have never felt good enough, never felt pretty enough, and never felt smart enough. We need faith in God to slay all the giants in our lives.

David's conquest over Goliath was only the beginning of a movement that led many of David's mighty men to slay many other giants and beasts by the power of the Holy Ghost.

> *[23]And he slew an Egyptian, a man of great stature, five cubits high. And in the Egyptian's hand was a spear like a weaver's beam; and he went down to him with a staff and plucked the spear out of the Egyptian's hand, and slew him with his own spear.*
>
> *(1 chronicles Ch.11 vv23 – 25)*

> *[24]These things did Benaiah the son of Jehoiada, and had a name among the three mighties.*

25Behold, he was honorable among the thirty, but attained not to the first three; and David set him over his guard.

There are those that have slayed giants, most importantly we have our Lord Jesus who obtained the most important victory throughout all of man's history.

Saviour

Tis dark, the night has risen
Men go about their works
Their secret acts, on a broad way
They walked through a broad gate
As water passes between the hands

Here he comes, with beautiful wings
Mighty in Power, glorious in majesty
Brightness greater than that of the sun
His countenance more fearful
Than the flow of lava

He has come with healing
He has brought us truth
He shines in our darkness
He lights our path
His day has arisen

The breaking forth of dawn
He died
That our night might end
He rose in the morning
That we would work while it's day

The greatness of His power
The fullness of His love
Bounteous grace, yet for us to comprehend
As plenteous snow, an ocean of rain
Great is the measure of His love

The rhythm of love, cadence of His heart
The beats of life, footsteps of the way
Warm as the sun in its strength
Comforting as oil on the skin
The God of promises

He is the saviour.

CHAPTER 7

The Hidden Dangers

Names and locations have been changed to protect the identities of the individuals in this story. Everything is not exactly as it has been told, but this story serves to illustrate a lesson. Their account is unfortunately not that rare, but it is laid bare here, to illustrate how we can fail even when our intention is to keep God's commandment. When we have believed in God's word, 'that instructions are the ways of life'.

Lenard's personal Story

Fall, fall, revive me
Wake me up, I want my own
My gifts that I should shine
Give me the stars
I want to be useful

To shine, to give light
Pour on me, oh rain where are you?
To grow, to become what He must
So I'll wait for the rain

For His touch
Even so, I'll rise

Lenard had arrived in Accra, he had come to work in the orphanage and the children's school not far from Korle-bu. Lennard had been Christian ever since he remembered, his main driving passion was making a difference in people's life and standing up for injustice. He arrived in Ghana, not exactly sure what God had in store for him, but with the knowledge that he would not return home to Toronto the same person. He was scheduled to be a volunteer for the next four weeks at the orphanage, then a week of tourism before flying back to Toronto. He had gladly taken a sabbatical from teaching for this purpose.

It was the month of August, and the weather was very humid in Accra, the work was very rewarding but Lenard was finding it a bit lonely after work. He used most of this time in praying and waiting on God. He usually woke up at 7am and started work at 8am, then worked through until about 5pm most evenings. Most of his tasks involved taking the little orphans to school, feeding those that couldn't feed themselves and assisting the visiting doctor in administering medication and treatments to the orphans or sometimes staff members that were sick. He spent his first week in this manner, but in the evenings he began to discover entertainment such as salsa dancing at Coconut grove. It proved to be fun in a relaxing atmosphere where he felt alive.

At the beginning of the second week, a new volunteer arrived from the United Kingdom. She was a medical student on a voluntary elective at Korle-bu medical school. She was staying at the international student accommodation hostels, but she chose to volunteer for two days at the orphanage each week. She came from a catholic home, was of mixed heritage but didn't consider herself particularly religious though she believed in God. She too immediately started to find her time very boring. Lenard met her on her first day of volunteering at the orphanage, which was the Wednesday of the second week since he had arrived.

They went to lunch together that afternoon where they ate meat pies and drank soft minerals after which they went to find the nearest cybercafé to check their Face-Book and emails. It was good to have found pleasant company at last on both sides. They were already beginning to find that they could only relate to the locals to a certain extent, besides which the locals were busy with the reality of their day to day lives. Before long they went everywhere together, and visited the national museum which displayed a lot of the historic art in Ghana, and took them through the history of the Ashanti tribe. They found out about the different costumes that the different tribes wore, and more importantly they learnt about the slave trade and the role that Ghana played in the slave trade.

Ghana was one of the slave ports that the slaves were brought to from all over West Africa; at different times the Dutch and the English were the Lord of the castle Sao Jorge in Elmina. They saw photos of the courtyard where they chained the slaves up while they waited to be taken from the soil of Africa. On Sundays above where the slaves were kept was the chapel where the slave masters had church. In the nights, the captain would stand above the courtyard to pick a slave maiden with whom he was to lay with that night.

Lenard was particularly touched on learning about the door of no return at the Elmina castle, which was the door that led unto the slave boats, for which the slaves that passed through were destined never to see or touch the soil of Africa again. Displayed in the museum were effigies of the different gods that the various tribes worshipped at different times. And then there were the recent carvings dedicated to 'Yahwey'.

Particularly striking was the ubiquitous carving of the Ashanti word 'Gye Nyame', which translated in English meant "except for God". Lennard was to find great meaning and comfort in these words in days that were to come. For he was to realize he couldn't stand 'gye nyame' (except for God). And just like the Ghanian people through their history had made a transition from serving idols to serving Yahwey, Lennard was to make the journey from operating in his own strength to operating by this new code 'gye nyame', I can do nothing.

The streets of Accra were very clean and decent, the people were humble and of a very quiet spirit. The ensuing days became more rewarding; they went to the cinema at Accra shopping mall and saw the recent movies. Although the medical student had a boyfriend back in the UK, she started to find that she was developing feelings for Lennard even though he wasn't her usual type, being very religious in her eyes. She was due to leave a week earlier than Lennard, so on her last weekend Lennard invited her to stay at the accommodation for the other volunteers as they were planning a series of outings that weekend.

They went to the Ghanaian beauty pageant show (Ghana's

most beautiful) with some of the other youth workers, and it was a lot of fun. On the last night they all went out to taste the night life in Accra, and while there on the dance-floor she kissed Lenard. They both thought it would end there. It so happened that on getting back to the accommodation, after everyone had walked to their rooms, Lenard walked her to her room as she didn't know where it was. Ignoring their instincts, they kissed goodnight, but they ended up spending the night together in her room.

Lenard didn't sleep for the rest of the night, he felt he was too weak and he had betrayed his God. She didn't understand his guilt and wanted to be with him. He didn't feel she was the right person for him, and had to apologize to her and deal with his feelings of guilt. Strangely the images in his head were those of the European forts, which were the oldest standing buildings in Ghana. The notion of slavery played on in his mind, and he vowed not to walk through the doors of no return.

In our present world, society (the majority) is always coercing us to be in rebellion against God, through the different ideas that are propagated in the media, they teach doctrines such as its okay to be a Christian and sleep with someone that you're in a relationship with but not married to. The hidden agenda is very effective, as Christians fall victim to this message and propaganda. They become full of shame, lacking authority and without power. They haven't learnt the lesson that integrity produces power, as my Pastor says. The church is unable to function in the place where it has the answers to society's ills because of its compromising the truth of God with the half-truth that the world is feeding it and at times challenging it with.

These are evidenced by the debate on abortion, on the legalisation of euthanasia. Even in more subtle things as in the content of sexual education teaching and when children should receive this. On every area of moral standing the church has been challenged by the world. At times the church has been told to stay out of these debates, with the argument that the church should not have a voice in the governance of a nation and even in determining its moral values. My question then is, if the church does not determine the moral stance of the nation, then who does? In Islamic societies, it is very clear that the moral norms and even most of the laws of these countries are based on the Quran. This is witnessed by women who have been killed for committing adultery, evidenced by the persecution of Christians and people of other religious beliefs in these communities.

The enemy never plays fair; he will kick you when you're down. He knows your weaknesses, he will hit you while you are down, come to you when you're weak. He loves it when the odds are stacked against you, when your social support is taken away, when your spiritual support seems far away, that's when the enemy loves to attack you. He is only interested in his victory over you and his ability to keep you in prison, he doesn't read fair play rule books, neither is he governed by any fair trade act. He is a saboteur, feeding on your weaknesses to strengthen his grip over you and sabotage your destiny. As such you shouldn't be amazed when he brings individuals or organizations into your associations who do not have a part in helping your dreams and God given destiny, but mostly unknown to them, their role is to distract you, detract from you and cause you to be unfulfilled. For I have been learning so recently; according to John Piper, author of 'Let the nations be glad', "God is most glorified when we're most satisfied in Him". I realize that my fulfilment comes from pleasing God and doing what He has tasked me to do. And this is the lesson that so many like Lenard need to learn.

My pastor once ministered on how the devil is like a fisher man. Just as how a fish is baited, so the enemy baits us, and at times we don't know that the bite of bait we are about to take is for our lives. We might nibble around the bait for a bit and think there are no strings attached. But the bait is attached to a tackle (i.e. a hook) which is attached to a line the fisherman uses in reeling the fish in. This is why it is important to be spiritually prepared, if not we do not think of the consequences of allowing ourselves to be baited by the enemy. For if we could foresee the consequences afterwards, we would not exchange our lives for a piece of bait.

I know better

We'll be exploring one of the other dangers that make one susceptible of falling foul of this hidden rebellion. I call it the ' I know better syndrome'. To define it simply, it is to think that you are qualified outside of God's truth, mandate, law and will to make any decision whatsoever pertaining to any sphere of your life. It's like the man that drinks alcohol because he likes drinking and negates that he is harming his body which is the temple of God by drinking too much. It is like the woman that eats too much because she can and she enjoys her food, and ignoring the damage she is doing to her health.

> *"For the kingdom of God is not a matter of eating and drinking, but of righteousness, peace and joy in the Holy spirit."*
>
> *(Rom Ch.14 vv17)*

This chapter is intended to question our lives, to challenge us on the areas which are not evidently sinful but when we chase after them according to our lust, we can actually call those behaviours by what they are, sin. We can talk about the sin of gluttony, the sin of alcoholism, basically the sin of putting anything above the precepts of God. It could be the fact that we care about our job more than we care about God, we care more about what society thinks than disciplining our children properly. From scriptures we know that the wise is not given to excess, wine is for mockers, for those who are so sorrowful that they need to forget their sorrows. Wise people are not given to gluttony, princes are not given to excess but they eat for strength.

> *"Blessed art thou, O land, when thy king is the son of nobles, and thy princes eat in due season, for strength, and not for drunkenness!"*
>
> *(Ecclessiastes Ch.10 vv17)*

> *"All things are lawful unto me, but all things are not expedient: all things are lawful for me, but I will not be brought under the power of any. Meats for the belly, and the belly for meats: but God shall destroy*

both it and them. Now the body is not for fornication,
but for the Lord: and the Lord for the body"
(I Corinthians Ch.5 vv12 – 13)

In what areas of our lives do we say that 'we know better' to God. Is it in our marriages, where we say we can become separated from one another or undergo divorce because of the issues in our marriage. Whereas in scriptures, there are clear instructions and criteria for separation and divorce. The idea of us knowing better only creates brokenness and pain in our relationships; we hurt and are maimed because of our rebellion. We are injured and start becoming malformed as the joints that have moved out of place are not being held in their rightful positions, so we end up walking with a limp. Then we fashion crutches to lean on, instead of returning to the healer, so that the broken bones can be put in to place and allowed to set, and the dislocated joints returned to their right position. Note the above statements are in reference to the brokenness of our hearts and our relationships.

" Defraud ye not one the other, except it be with
consent for a time, that ye may give yourselves to
fasting and prayer; and come together again, that
Satan tempt you not for your incontinency."
(1 Corinthians Ch7 vv5)

The deceit of Self Atonement

In Ghanain Trokosi tradition, it was the custom of these people to give young girls to the priests in servitude to the priests. Virgin young girls were given to the village priests as a means of appeasing the gods for crimes committed by family members, the girls were essentially slaves to the village priests. They worked on the farm, and were made to carry out domestic chores such as cooking and washing, they were regarded as the property of the village priests and had to be replaced if they died. Once these girls started menstruation, their enslavement also involved sexual servitude, in fact some sources have reported that the girls had no choice on when they had sex and with whom they had sex in the shrines of these priests.

Thankfully the charity group 'Equality' launched a campaign for the banning of this practice by the Ghanain government. This practice has now been outlawed and it contradicts some Acts in the Ghanain constitution such as the personal liberty, human acts and acts of freedom. As far as I know there are still reports of 'Trokosi servitude practice' in Ghana, and there are even those who oppose its banning saying it is the culture of these people.

Among the Trokosi, there have been a form of self atonement which was ingrained as part of their culture, the village priests choosing the female gender as their object, because it would provide a means for their sexual gratification. As far as 2002, there was still ongoing work as far as I know to eradicate Trokosi servitude practice. I will now attempt to tackle this issue from another angle.

My father was a traditionalist, even though he claimed faith in Jesus. He at times engaged in offering animal sacrifices and pouring out drink offerings to the ancestors and elders, beckoning them to pray for him and come to his aid and the aid of his family. As a child I remember him causing my immediate elder brother, whom he took the most pride in to wear his hat, sit on a stool and to pour out drink offerings to his ancestors, offering a prayer before each outpouring of ogogoro (strong alcoholic brew). Then he would take a sip of it saying this is for me, and pour out a drink speaking in my traditional language (Urhobo) that this is for you my father. He often began his prayers by asking for forgiveness.

In these prayers to his ancestors, my father usually wore a look of solemnity. And he was always glad when he could get us to participate, we especially didn't mind in participating in the drinking of this strong alcoholic spirit. He often went on to make prayers for himself, asking his fathers to protect him, to protect his family and to prosper him. On considering this matter, as the drink was poured onto the floor for the ancestors to drink from, it is a wonder why the ancestors and forefathers will only drink from the floor, and why they would only grant prayers after they've had a drink.

At other times he sacrificed animals. In my recollection; once he sacrificed a monkey, another time a dog, another time a cat, another time a pair of pigeons. Sometimes the sacrifices involved slaughtering the animals. At other times it involved offering the dead animal as a burnt sacrifice; sometimes the sacrifices were done outside the house, perhaps at an outside shrine. Some times when these sacrifices were made, he obliged us to eat some of the meat. When my elder brothers became born again Christians, they refused to partake of such meat. He punished them by throwing them out of the house. As a young Christian, I was about eight or nine years of age at this time.

There came a time when he made it his business to know whether I ate of this meat or not. To put this into perspective my father had eighteen or more other children, and three wives living in the house. I refused to eat this meat and ran away while my dad was at work. I knew he was going to be very angry and was afraid of how he was going to punish me. I eventually had to come back home, I came at a time I knew he wasn't going to be at home and I stayed in my room until morning praying he would forget. For I remembered that he had already dealt severely with my elder Christian brothers

He didn't forget, as soon as he was well awake he called for me, I came into the living room trembling with fear. Then he asked me, did you eat the meat and I said no, before I could explain, his face convulsed with anger as he grabbed me, picked me up and held me up in the air as if he was about to dash me to the ground, I was indeed terrified at this point. Then all of a sudden his anger abated enough and he put me to the ground, and warned me that I must partake of the next sacrificed meat.

My father was a very rich man at a time, but we believe (me and my siblings) that as a result of these beliefs and such practices he shared, in addition to marrying several wives he lost everything. Living in my father's house, it seemed like there was an oppressor in the house. An oppressor, who required sacrifices; but was unable to deliver us or provide for us, to my knowledge he has only funded only one of his many children through university.

There remains the burden of poverty over my family and a lack of success seems to be the general rule. My elder siblings started to realize, that for them to break through they had to leave the house.

I believe we're slowly realizing the breaking of these yokes and burdens, a few of them have been able to get married and have children in their own homes, finish studying at university, get good paying jobs and enter their chosen career path. And it seems that for those that have remained in the house, it is as though they are almost in stagnation or regression.

I share this personal story, because for me it shows how useless every atonement sacrifice we offer is. Whether we openly sacrifice to other gods, whether we try to atone for our own sins, hoping we can make up for them. I would like to remonstrate again, that because we can get people to follow us in our rebellions, it doesn't make it right. God proves Himself true, as we realize that the blood of animals, not even our blood could free us and give us life. But only the blood of His son Jesus Christ, praise be to God the Father.

> *"For it is not possible that the blood of bulls and of goats should take away sins. Wherefore when He cometh into the world, he saith, sacrifice and offering thou wouldest not, but a body hast thou prepared me: In burnt offerings and sacrifices for sin thou hast no pleasure. Then said I, Lo, I come (in the volume of the book it is written of me,) to do thy will, O God."*
>
> *(Hebrews Ch.10 vv4 -7)*

(Verses 9-10) "Then said he, Lo, I come to do thy will, O God. He taketh away the first that he may establish the second. By the which will we are sanctified through the offering of the body of Jesus Christ once for all."

Just like it was with the Israelites, there were times when they turned and served the gods of the surrounding nations, like the Amonites and the Moabites. One of these gods was Molech, and one of the sacrifices Molech required was for its followers to offer their children as a sacrifice by fire. God reminded the Israelites the burden that is placed on them when they serve other gods, for God indeed would never ask such sacrifices of us. The burdens placed on us by the gods of this world are too heavy, too costly and too irrational. We don't have to offer our children as burnt offerings. The good news is we don't have to serve these gods and they definitely do not have any power over us.

Scripture clearly makes us to understand that there was no other sacrifice good enough. Godly sorrow leads to repentance; we should not remain at the place where guilt of the past eats at us and cause us to beat ourselves up. Our worth in the eyes of God is not determined by the righteous acts we do, or the failings of our past or present. It is based solely on His love for us; however our destinies are created by our obedience and submission to the will of God.

Judas' example

After Judas Iscariot betrayed the Lord Jesus Christ he was sorry and full of regret. He was also ashamed of what he had done. Now he could see that the devil had lied to him and blinded his heart from the truth. Though he had been with Jesus these three and a half years, yet he did not understand the purpose of the Messiah, he clearly didn't have a true revelation of who Jesus was, because if he did he would not have betrayed him.

Judas had waited for Jesus to rise up and take the physical kingdom of Israel back to Himself, he misunderstood that the Messiah was truly a king who would rule forever as Jacob had prophesied in the book of Genesis when he spoke of the sceptre not departing from Judah until it comes to 'Shiloh' to whom it belongs. Judas instead thought the kingdom of Christ was an earthly one; it would seem to us that Judas had jumped aboard with Jesus to fulfil his own vision and desires to see Israel wrestled from the hand of the Roman Empire via supernatural means. However God doesn't reason like we do, if he understood scripture he would understand that God is not for his ideals nor for the Roman ideal. Even today, God is not on my side, nor on anybody's side.

The purpose of this book is to announce that God is on His own side, we can see this through scripture. In Joshua 5, Joshua confronts the Captain of the host of the Lord's army and asks him, are you for us or against us?

"And it came to pass, when Joshua was by Jericho, that he lifted up his eyes and looked, and, behold, there stood a man over against him with his sword drawn in his hand: and Joshua went unto him, and said unto him, Art thou for us, or for our adversaries? And he said, Nay; but as captain of the host of the

Lord am I now come. And Joshua fell on his face to the earth, and did worship, and said unto him, what saith my lord unto his servant? And the captain of the Lord's host said unto Joshua, Loose thy shoe from off thy foot; for the place whereon thou standest is holy, and Joshua did so."

(Joshua Ch.5 vv13 -15)

The lesson here is as I mentioned before, God is not for our agenda or schemes. But He is working in the earth for His purpose, and He has revealed Himself unto us today, asking us to fall inline. He is calling us into divine order, where those who serve before Him walk in Godly fear. He says to us, take off your shoe, for the place where you stand is holy ground. In other words, He has called you to a holy calling, and His presence is holy, so that we can have no security in standing in anything that comes from us, but rather that we stand honest in His presence. The other important lesson here is that as we are in His presence we should recognize His authority. He is the Lord of the hosts, and is authority is over everything. Judas didn't recognize this sovereignty although he stood daily in the presence of the Lord of host for the space of three and a half years. He didn't realize that his ideas, desires, opinions, thoughts and plans were to bow in obedience and honour to the King and Lord of the hosts.

Is there any time in our lives we feel that "Lord it is okay for me to have the final say on this matter. It is my place not to submit and discard my will, thoughts, desires and plans when it doesn't line up with yours". This is the rebellion I'm talking about, and the ending of this rebellion is not where we ask the Lord if He is on our side, but when we bow and say Lord I'm on your side and like a good soldier, I'm falling in line! I am coming into divine order!

This was Judas' rebellion, of not submitting his will to Christ's desire to fulfil the work the father sent Him to do. So Judas sinned, but he found no room for repentance. Judas was condemned because of his rebellious act, and his inability to allow himself to be broken by God. Even after he betrayed Christ there was still hope for salvation for him, just like there was for Peter (Cephas). He fulfilled the first step, he was sorry, and then he became full of shame and regret. These to some extent are natural emotions of being sorry for making a mistake. However Judas remained in a place of regret, which wasn't God's desire for him. His sorrow was not of a Godly sort.

Let us read from *Matthew 27:*

> *"Then Judas, which had betrayed him, when he saw that he was condemned, repented himself, and brought again the thirty pieces of silver to the chief priests and elders, saying, I have sinned in that I have betrayed the innocent blood. And they said, what is that to us? See thou to that. And he cast down the pieces of silver in the temple, and departed, and went and hanged himself. And the chief priest took the silver pieces, and said, it is not lawful for to put them into the treasury, because it is the price of blood." (verses 3-6)*

So when he realized he had sinned, he tried to pay his way back, realized he couldn't so took his own life. Our intentions might seem good, but they cannot justify our actions. Would we attempt to continue to offer our own sacrifices, drowning ourselves in good deeds or acts of penitence to earn some form of right standing with God? God sets the requirements, and He has offered His son Christ Jesus as a sacrifice once and for all, for all debts owed. This is an answer to questions some people might have, there is no other way to God but by Jesus Christ, we cannot amend, omit or add to God's requirement which is simple faith in the Lord Jesus Christ.

Doubt

At times you hear news of coming and present destruction, and the enemy asks you "who is the Lord that you should trust Him"?

One thing I've been learning in my experiential relationship with God is learning to trust Him based on what He has done for me in the past. The bible urges us to learn from the patriarchs of faith and to follow their examples. I dared to believe God when I gave my life to Jesus and I dared to trust that His words and promises were all true and I wasn't disappointed. Without making that first step I would never have been able to experience the truth of His word, they would have just been empty words to me.

> "And I said. This is my infirmity: but I will remember the years of the right hand of the most High. I will remember the works of the Lord: surely I will remember thy wonders of old. I will meditate

also of all thy work, and talk of thy doings. Thy
way, O God, is in the sanctuary: who is so great a
God as our God? Thou art the God that doest
wonders: thou hast declared thy strength among the
people. Thou hast with thine arm redeemed thy
people, the sons of Jacob and Joseph. Selah".

(Psalm Ch.77 vv10 – 15)

This is the case for all who have believed, they trusted despite not seeing with their eyes.

"Jesus saith unto him, Thomas, because thou hast
seen me, thou hast believed: blessed are they that
have not seen, and yet have believed."

(John Ch.20 vv29)

We trusted God and God proved Himself, and He continues to do wonders time and time again. We can recount this through the Old Testament.

He sent plagues on Egypt and then rescued Israel, leading them through the red sea by dividing it with the breath of His word. He gave them water to drink from a rock in the wilderness; for forty years He led them by a pillar of cloud by day and a pillar of fire by night. When the Israelites were oppressed, He raised up Jepthah, Gideon, Samson, and the prophet Samuel to deliver them. He gave Esther favour before King Ahaseurus that the nation of Israel was not wiped out, He rescued Daniel from the lion's den, He brought the children of Israel from captivity.

As if that was not enough He caused the nation that held

Israel captive to aid in rebuilding the temple and the walls of Jerusalem, He caused Israel to dwell in peace and safe from enemies on all sides, because of His great love.

In the New Testament, He sent His only begotten son Jesus Christ into the world, making the virgin birth possible. He fed the five thousand, He walked on water, He raised up the dead, He spoke from heaven audibly as recorded three times in the gospel. The first was in at the baptism of Jesus, He spoke to Jesus again in the hearing of people and the Pharisees claimed it was thunder and He declared His love and pleasure in His son on the Mount of Transfiguration. He gave His son the Christ for the sins of the whole world, which He had created in the first instance.

> *"For God is my King of old, working salvation in the midst of the earth. Thou didst divide the sea by thy strength: thou brakest the heads of the dragons in the waters. Thou brakest the heads of leviathan in pieces, and gavest him to be meat to the people inhabiting the wilderness. Thou didst cleave the fountain and the flood: thou driedst up mighty rivers. The day is thine, the night also is thine: thou hast prepared the light and the sun. Thou hast set all the borders of the earth: thou hast made summer and winter."*
> *(Psalm Ch.74 vv12 – 17)*

Now is there a question to ask, 'what can He not do?' or 'what will He not do?' I hope you can see that there is absolutely nothing impossible for Him, and that there is no length He won't go to in order to deliver you. He has shown and He still is in the business of delivering all His children from the effects of evil and the afflictions of the evil one. Is there an evil or negative situation in your life you are questioning if God will deliver you from? He is willing, He fully demonstrated His willingness by spreading His arms out wide on the cross, and He is able.

"For the earth is the Lord's and its fullness thereof, the world and they that dwell therein"
(Psalm Ch.24 vv1).

We might say so this is what God has done in the bible, but I can say God is still in act of demonstrating He is bigger than every mountain I can or cannot see. He fed the 5000 with a few fishes and loaves, He walked on the water, He healed the blind, cured the leper, raised the dead, He rose Himself from the dead; surely anyone that can do that is able! I'm just exalting God in these passages, or rather making it plain that God is exalting Himself continually through His acts and His word! His sole interest is the pursuit of His own glory and He is very jealous of it, that He would not give His honour to anyone else. Even His love for you, is a revelation, an exultation of His goodness. As God is infinitely good and holy and righteous, He can only do the right thing by promoting Himself (as He is all that is God).

"Thus saith the Lord the King of Israel, and his redeemer the Lord of hosts: I am the first, and I am the last: and beside me there is no God. And who as I, shall call, and shall declare it, and set it in order for me, since I appointed the ancient people? And the things that are coming, and shall come, and let them shew unto them."
(Isaiah Ch.44 vv6-7)

111

(Verse 24) *"Thus saith the Lord, thy redeemer, and he that formed thee from the womb, I am the Lord that maketh all things; that stretcheth forth the heavens alone: that spreadeth abroad the earth by myself".*

In my life I can testify of His goodness, He brought me to this world, He saved my life from sickness and death multiple times as a child. Once I was ill as a child and it turned out that apparently I had been walking around with haemoglobin (blood count level) count of 6. The normal range is round about above 12, yet I was alive and did everything that other kids did. I was taken to hospital when my mum arrived from the UK and was concerned about me. He provided for me all my life; even when my parents had no money. He brought me to my current location in England, He caused me to graduate from medical school, He provided for me for all the trips I needed to make for my studies, even though my mum didn't have a job. He has kept me from evil and from being consumed even by my own lusts. Then he gave me dreams and visions when I had none, and He anointed me and is still reconciling me to himself as I continue to seek His presence. I know there is nothing my God cannot do.

Given such compelling evidence, I have no grounds for doubt; I cannot make room for doubt. You cannot make room for doubt, it's time to kick doubt out of the door and allow faith to rise up. Doubt is the enemy's weapon for causing you to limit the immortal God who is able and willing to bring about that which is good and perfect in and for your life. I hope you see the danger of doubt. I hope that you would embrace faith as your sister, so that you and also those that are waiting for you might obtain of the promises that God has made concerning you.

Ignorance of Sin's power

Sin separates us from God; sin destroys the relationships we have with one another. We hurt one another because we sin against one another. We are angry against one another because we sin against one another. Our relationships die because we keep repeating offences. For example a man keeps cheating on His wife even though she forgave him once before. A compulsive thief who has escaped many times, without anyone knowing he was a thief until he got caught because he couldn't stop stealing. The child abuser who had offended hundreds of times, but was finally caught because he was a slave to his/her evil inclinations. Even the guy that keeps driving without a license till the police stopped and fined him.

Sin is a taskmaster and makes us its slave as soon as we obey it. Then it begins the process of killing us. Its end is death, sometimes slowly, sometimes quickly. Sometimes openly as when a murderer is publicly executed for his/her murders in countries that allow capital punishment, or sometimes silently and secretly as when a person dies from cancer from smoking, from AIDS from fornicating. Even more, sin not only affects the individuals, it affects our families, our churches, our society, our government, even our future. Only the blood of Jesus can stop sin with its murderous intentions. Taking the prior point that sin not only affects the individual, we can see this in children born with aids, deformed and small babies born to mothers who are addicted to cigarettes, alcohol and drugs.

Children born to mothers who smoke are smaller than those born to non-smoking mothers, they also have smaller brains. Studies have shown smoking is a risk factor for miscarriages; it causes infertility and complications during pregnancy. As regards to alcohol, heavy drinking can affect the development of the baby's organs leading to malformation and developmental abnormalities, alcohol also puts the baby at risk of developing foetal alcohol spectrum disorder which is a lifelong disorder.

There still remains many sorrowful tales of people who have suffered great loss as a consequence of self abuse. Daily we walk by some homeless people begging on the streets, some of them had productive lives until they started self-medicating certain pains in their life with alcohol, then things spiralled out of control. Would it be surprising to think that some of these homeless people might have been high-flying professionals, they could be ex-servicemen who served their country on the frontline of many battles for the freedom we now enjoy and the agenda of the UK. Returning from war but unable to cope with its scars, or the demands of returning to a civilian life.

Taking it further, the lives of many stars have been ruined by an obsession or an addiction. It seems like their names go on and on. I can think of Michael Jackson, dead at the age of 50, from a propofol overdose, of Amy Winehouse; allegedly dead at the tender age of 27 from alcohol intoxication. Also more recently of 48 year old Whitney Houston who had battled all her life with drugs, and was found dead in a bathtub in Los Angeles, allegedly from an accidental overdose of prescription medicines (February 2012). In my opinion, all too young to die, exceptional talents with more to offer the world. The world mourns their passing, and looks upon it as a great loss. Even yet there are many whose sad story remains untold.

Continuing with my accusation of the oppression of sin, we can see it, in laws that make it compulsory for everyone to have car insurance. The law is not evil, it is there to protect those who are law abiding from those that are not. We can also see this in the security checks at the airports before getting unto the plane, because the threat of terrorism is very real. I remember a personal episode clearly. Not long after the bombing attacks in London (07/July/2005), I was escorting a friend some of the way home. She had come to visit me from Reading, as she was due to be flying to the United States to stay permanently. As we said our goodbyes at the underground station, we decided to take a picture. As soon as we had taken the picture, we were confronted by two policemen, who informed us that flash photography or taking pictures on the underground was not allowed. We were not arrested or cautioned, but this story is just an illustration of how simple liberties can be curtailed because of other people's terrorist acts.

> *"For what the law could not do, in that it was weak through the flesh, God sending his own Son in the likeness of sinful flesh, and for sin, condemned sin in the flesh: That the righteousness of the law might be fulfilled in us, who walk not after the flesh, but after the spirit."*
>
> *(Rom Ch.8 vv3-4)*

We have belittled the significance of sin and made it a trivial matter. Our world has become a marketplace for sin, a common place for iniquity and a closet for unrighteousness. In fact unrighteousness has become our personal affair. Our trivial affair with sin could be due to our lack of fear of God, our thought in not affirming that He truly is sovereign. To defeat sin, we really need to meditate on God's sovereignty, as recognising it, causes us to fall on Him and rely on Him in time of need. God's word tells us that ' the fear of the Lord is the beginning of wisdom, the knowledge of the most High is the beginning of understanding'.

When we start to entertain sin in our minds, we begin to make it less vile in our minds. We endeavour to dress it up, so it doesn't paint such an ugly picture in our conscience. The vileness and rottenness of sin will often return to stun our minds, when guilt sets in after an act of disobedience. We become sorrowful with shame, that we allowed ourselves to entertain something so truly vile and ugly. Rationalizing with sin doesn't lessen its consequences.

By looking to God, we cease to measure by our own standards, which are crooked and inadequate. We desist from trying to please others, living for others, desiring the praise and certification of others. Rather we desire the sealing of God's Spirit; we come to the place where we answer with a clear conscience to God. We live by God's standards, we seek to please God and we bow to God's word! Our God is truly in the act of reconciling the rebellious heart back to Himself.

The idea of belittling God, the 'I know better syndrome'.

The extent to which blame can be apportioned to an individual comes from how high the dignity you offended and not how long you've been offending. We can argue this out; in the home you'll be looked on and punished more severely for being rude to your parents than being rude to your siblings. It is a greater crime with greater punishment for you to assault a member of the royal family than if you assaulted a common civilian. This is important to recognise in understanding the supremacy of God and the severity of His judgements. In knowing God, we understand more, and see clearer how sin is an abomination to Him, but righteousness is His delight. As God is far greater than all, are we able to agree with Him, the extent to which we truly have offended? And the punishment we deserve in considering that He is the God that is higher than all else.

Blame

At times I feel as though we act like we can get God to do what we want. It might be that we're saying "Lord if you do not do this for me, I'm going to do that and I'm not going to do that". And I hear the master saying 'why do you call me Lord and do not do what I say?' We are not necessarily overt in saying this or behaving in this way. It is true to say if some thieves had money they would not steal; despite them stealing out of need it does not put them in the right.

We have excuses for the way we act; I cannot forgive him unless he comes to beg for it. I cannot pay my tithes because things are hard. I cannot help the poor because I don't have enough money. I cannot plead the cause of the widow and the orphans because those who oppress them are strong, I cannot do that which is right because I am weak. If we are weak in the times of adversity, then our strength is truly small.

In essence we say to God I cannot do what you say because I'm under pressure not to. We forget that God knows we are under pressure and He commands us, He beckons to us to obey Him despite this. His primary interest is in our obedience to His will. He is able to deal with the pressure, the fact that you're hungry, the fact that you have debts, the fact that people have hurt you, the fact that you're persecuted without cause, the fact that your resources are limited. To put it even better He allowed this circumstances to prove what was inside of us.

Whether it has to do with us rationalizing our use of bad language and swear words because we are movie stars, and that's what we do for a living, or we are musicians and we know that sex sells. So we have to sing about sex, we have to have sexy videos, even on gospel recordings. In short we do what it takes. If this is our rationale, the question we should ask ourselves is this, 'are we trying to draw people to ourselves or are we interested in pleasing God?'

Let us go to the book of Judges, so that we can see that God is aware of the opposition that we face. Opposition and enemies, hardship and difficulties, none of these should be excuses for us to disobey or be rebellious.

> *"Now these are the nations which the Lord left, to prove Israel by them, even as many of Israel as had*

not known all the wars of Canaan. Only that the generations of the children of Israel might know, to teach them war, at least such as before knew nothing thereof."

(Judges Ch.3 vv1-2)

In these verses, we can suggest that God wants to test us, in that whatever is inside us should be revealed, that the things which are secret in us might be shown up whether good or bad. Secondly he wants us to learn to fight, for there are many of us that have not understood war. When we think on this we see clearly that we are in a battlefield and God wants us to learn to battle so that we might become like our master (Saviour) who rides out to conquer and conquer until he brings everything under subjection unto Himself. Think upon this statement in reference to the section on being spiritually prepared. We can be like the Captain of our faith because, as mentioned previously our victory is already assured, for Christ has already conquered. The Lord is reminding us that in war He is with us, in the daily wars of our relationships, marriages, jobs, soul winning, He is with us if we are subservient to Him.

Sin is a common problem, it leaves its mark and it can scar.

"And of whom hast thou been afraid or feared, that thou hast lied, and hast not remembered me, nor laid it to thy heart? Have not I held my peace even of old, and thou fearest me not?" Verse 15 - for thus saith the high and lofty One that inhabiteth eternity, whose name is Holy, I dwell in the high and holy

place, with him also that is of a contrite and humble spirit, to revive the spirit of the humble, and to revive the heart of the contrite one."

(Isaiah Ch.57 vv11)

CHAPTER 8

An Hour of Darkness

In June 1967, the Israelites recorded a famous victory in the 'Six day War'. In which they defeated four Arab nations, the main Arab powers at that time. Prior to this war there was growing fear and apprehension in Israel as they faced threats on all sides. The war was fought against Syria, Iraq, Jordan and Egypt.

There are many views held about why this war took place and how Israel was able to attain victory against these powerful Arab states. Prior to the war, terrorism against Israel had been rife, ever since Israel had become established as a state following the holocaust. There were 35 terrorist attacks on Israel in 1965, 41 in 1966, and in the first four months of 1967 there had already been 37 terrorist attacks. Even today there are still numerous terror attacks against Israel, mainly from neighbouring Palestine, plus Israel is continually verbally threatened by powerful Arab states like Iran.

The Syrian army were also in the habit of shelling Israeli villages from the Golan Heights. Israel complained to the United Nations; however the Soviet Union used their veto, to prevent any action from being taken to prevent Syrian's aggression. It was at this time Syria began to demand open and all out war against Israel (Near East report, Tigay 1980). Syrian attacks and Israel's response to these attacks caused Syria to prompt Egypt to support them.

A series of events occurred to place Israel in greater jeopardy. In May 1967, Egypt made it clear to the United Nations that they had to leave the Suez region where they acted as international peace keepers. The Suez Canal was the only direct means of transport between the Mediterranean and Indian Ocean. In earlier years the UN had stepped in to ensure Britain and France returned control of the canal back to Egypt when the Egyptians blocked the canal by sinking 40 ships in it.

Notably, Israel was only then 19 years old, having become a state again in 1948. The youngest survivors of the holocausts were barely in their 20s. Israel was then being pressed beyond measure, being faced with the threat of extinction at the turn of every decade. Israel had been in this situation before, although I have no idea if the young Israelis at that time (1967) remembered. During the reign of Ahasuerus, emperor of the provinces of Persia and Media, Hamann had tried to use manipulation to get the emperor Ahasuerus to wipe Israel out, but God saved Israel through Queen Esther (as recorded as in the book of Esther). This occurred sometime between 486 – 465 BC.

Its enemies at this time were making statements such as "We have nothing for Israel except war – comprehensive war ... marching against its gangs, destroying and putting an end to the whole Zionist existence.., every one of the 100 million Arabs has been living for the past 19 years on one hope – to live to die on the day that Israel is liquidated".

Egypt provoked and threatened Israel further by, moving her forces into the 'Saini desert', Cairo radio announced that all Egypt was now preparing to plunge into total war which will put an end to Israel. The UN complied with Egypt's request allowing Cairo radio to announce "As of today, there no longer exist any international emergency force to protect Israel. We shall exercise patience no more, we shall not complain any more to the UN about Israel. The sole method we shall apply against Israel is a total war which will result in the extermination of Zionist existence."

'Though we're few we're surrounded by many, who have crossed that river'.

Above are the words from Don Moen's song, 'Our Father'. I usually like to add to the end of this that 'we've prospered like never before'. In this paraphrased line, lies a prophecy about the people of God. For when we are surrounded by our enemies, when they have established a confederacy and a coalition amongst themselves to thwart us, to annihilate or destroy us, it was then that we broke through. The words from Don Moen's song also speaks of the cloud (great number of saints and patriarchs) of witnesses who have overcome such great opposition as we face now. For God has apportioned it to be a season in which we prospered and broke through. It is also a reminder that the things we're going through are not unique to us as people of God, but that we can receive comfort in that there are many that have been before us that have experienced like struggles and had overcome. For we do indeed have a great cloud of witnesses with us.

The above account does not seek to explain why Israel prospered in this battle but to show the work of God in our lives. Israel's defence minister initiated a pre-emptive attack on the Arab coalition, starting on the 5th of June and ending on the 10th of June 1967. They defeated the surrounding nations, bringing the Arab world to shame and temporarily weakening them.

"For this is the song we'll be singing forever, 'Holy is the Lord". The preceding sentence is another line from the song 'Our Father'. In essence this song captures the message I'm bringing to you in this book. We are crying for God's mercy, acknowledging His splendour and declaring our need for Him.

As a consequence of this war, Israel captured the Sinai Peninsula and the Gaza strip from Egypt, the Golan Heights from Syria, and the West Bank and East Jerusalem from Jordan (BBC news). News reports at that time claimed that "the Israeli generals... had been training to finish the unfinished business of Israel's war of 1948 – the capture of East Jerusalem – for most of their careers". The important consequence was that civilian Israelis who believed they were doomed at the peak of these threats, were now relieved. The Jews believe that God saved them and reunited them with their historic homeland in Judea and Samaria.

There have been other times of darkness, not too long before this, just preceding and during the Second World War. The Nazis working under the idea of Lebensraum (meaning living space or habitat) – their idea was that as the naturally superior species they were to make space for themselves by wiping out the peoples in the lands where they were planning to settle themselves, so including Poland. They also extended the breadth of their idea, that it became their habit to kill people they considered handicapped or unfit. These included the Jews, the physically and mentally disabled, Jehovah witnesses whom they considered as religious deviants, Poles and others besides. They sent them to camps for forced labour or extermination.

It is noteworthy that their work started with only a little tint of racism. From putting Jews out of work and business, banning them from selling, stopping them from eating in the same public houses as Germans, forcing them to wear a yellow star to identify themselves, it extended to annihilating 6 million Jews in the concentration camps. The word holocaust is of Greek origin, and means 'sacrifice by fire'.

My writing is not about the plight of Jews, it is about the darkness that seems to be present in our world today that seems strong and so vicious. That starts off by entering in through cracks, then proceeding to take over and cover everything in its hateful blackness. The beginning of the holocaust was perpetuated by the Nazi Idea, based on myths and imaginations that the Jews were trying to systemically take over the world.

Darkness in today's World

It seems that the darkness is near and never too far away,

at times our minds could be in a place where we are waiting for the next atrocity to come on the news, waiting for the next disaster to flash across our television screens. We live in a time where generations are systematically oppressed and exploited, where famine ravages developing countries, when tsunamis and earthquakes claim lives and cause unspoken destruction. There are numerous example, one current situation that hasn't been given enough attention in regards to action being taken to save a people from a manmade disaster is the one in the Democratic Republic of Congo. It is more than about 'Coltan', a natural resource which is found in many of our electrical equipment and mobile phones.

In our generation, official statistics show a rise in knife crimes, and stabbing related deaths. Particularly in London (UK) there has been a rise in the number of young black males who have been stabbed to death by other young people mostly of ethnic minority origin. We might be able to put a number to the number of young people whose lives have been claimed by knife crime in the UK, in the last 5 years, but we have the inability to measure their grief, as it appears the effect of this darkness has reached many families.

Throughout human history and especially more recently we hear of and experience tragedy caused by natural disasters. I'm not expanding on those tragedies in this chapter. Despite their magnitude, we've had earthquakes in Japan, floods in numerous places, famine in Somalia and other parts of Eastern Africa. These events have affected the lives of many, but at times the media can make us numb to the conditions and pain of its victims.

What this chapter is particularly concerned about is about the idea that wickedness seems to be in high places. That those who perpetuate cruelty, and wickedness have power on their side. There have been many examples of mass murder and evil dealings in our modern world. We remember the 1994 genocide in Rwanda where about 800,000 people were murdered in the space of just 100 days. In some estimates, the numbers equate to murdering of about 20% of the country's population.

Neither have we forgotten the use of child soldiers in Sierra Leone's civil war, as the world witnessed how the small political leaders manipulated children into becoming killing machines. These acts not only occur in the developing world, but are also perpetuated by individuals, groups, and governments in the developed world. A newspaper clipping from 2009 shows that British based oil traders have dumped toxic in the Ivory Coast waste including hydrogen sulphide, a highly toxic compound that can kill. Thousands, even millions of people were reported to have fallen ill or died; the effect was so severe that it overwhelmed the country's health resource.

In the last couple of years the media has highlighted the working conditions within Chinese companies. This was brought to the world's attention by a spate of employee suicides. In 2010, there were at least 10 employee suicide deaths at the Chinese company 'Foxconn'. One employee cited intolerable working condition, at the company that produces computer parts and other equipments for large companies such as Hewlett Packard, Apple and Sony Ericsson.

"Wherefore do the wicked live, become old, yea, are

mighty in power? Their seed is established in their sight with them, and their offspring before their eyes. Their houses are safe from fear, neither is the rod of God upon them. Their bull gendereth, and faileth not: their cow calveth, and casteth not her calf. They send forth their little ones like a flock, and their children dance. They take the timbrel and harp, and rejoice at the sound of the organ. They spend their days in wealth, and in a moment go down to the grave. Therefore they say unto God, Depart from us: for we desire not the knowledge of thy ways. What is the Almighty that we should serve him? And what profit should we have, if we pray unto him?"

(Job 21 vs 7 – 15)

Do the sentiments of Job while in his affliction echo in our heart? Are there times we feel that the wicked prospers and innocent people suffer for it? Because they prosper, they feel they have no need of God. Looking at it from another perspective they prosper because of oppression, because they've made someone else uncomfortable, because they have taken away somebody's income so that the person is unable to feed their family. This is part of the problem in DR Congo; there have been reports that countries such as the United States operate through countries such as Rwanda and Uganda to forcefully extract some of the natural resources of the country. Congo lies in the heart of Africa and is probably the most mineral resource rich country in Africa. To get to these natural resources, alleged Rwandan and Uganda rebel armies have driven out the indigenous people of these parts, killing some and raping the women.

The truth is the indigenous people of Congo cannot eat tin, copper or coltan. However they do need their houses to live in, they need the ground for farming. If the world wants their resources why doesn't the world just ask them instead of using a cruel system of control to obtain these resources?

They do not suffer the ill effect that the weak suffer because they've dumped their toxic waste in the poor man's field, because they know the poor is unable to contend with them, whether in a court of law or in any other form. They can get away with paedophilia, murder, rape, and lying in court because there is wealth and power on their side.

Bringing this into perspective, it is not an attack on rich people, neither on the governments of the world. Other different examples of these are the imbalance we have in some of the laws in the land. For example there is a recent case that the GMC (General Medical Council) has brought against a Christian doctor (23 September 2011). A patient, under encouragement from a mother, made a complaint against him of preaching to her during an appointment in his surgery, in which the patient was considering using the emergency contraceptive pill. Despite the fact that the patient has not presented herself or turned up at the hearing the GMC have still decided to pursue a case against this doctor. The injustice is that in every case there should always be the opportunity to cross-examine the witness. The Christian concern will state ' without the chance to cross examine, every doctor becomes very vulnerable to accusations from patients', as all GP consultations are one to one.

Moving the discussion ever closer to a Christian perspective.

We are in the era when prayer has been banned from schools in America; basically the government has sent a message to God. ' Keep out of our schools'. Is it any wonder over the years that our governments continue to pursue agendas that lead to a growing number of atheists and many that dishonour God in the world? In England more recently many "Christian schools" are contemplating the idea of no longer having Christian assemblies. Our children learn a lot from school and are greatly influenced by the ideas that they are taught in school. It is thought that after the age of five children are most influenced by their teachers. But here we see the message that the government keeps leaving for God, 'Stay out of our schools'.

According to a survey conducted for the 'Richard Dawkins Foundation – For reason and science (UK)', published in 2012. 74% of Christians agree that religion should not affect public policy. However Baroness Warsi, a cabinet office minister argues on the contrary, that 'Faith needs "a seat at the table in public life". In another recent ruling, a high court judge recently outlawed the century old tradition of formal prayers being said at the beginning of council meetings.

Many will act as though God is the problem; others will even go as far as belittling Him, liking Him to an idea that is in a particular subset of the population. They are trying to shut Him up, trying to cage Him, trying to box Him out of our lives and our society. The truth is that we are the problem and God is the solution. In the aftermath of September 11 2001, people didn't wait for an order from the government before they started offering prayers in schools and everywhere else. I hope this helps us to understand what Job's complaint about the wicked was, when he speaks "Therefore they say unto God, depart from us, for we desire not the knowledge of your ways", for we have no need of you (God).

Many who have no belief in God; say He is an idea created in our minds. They say the human mind is a powerful thing and we that have faith need to ascribe the things that are to a cause. As some claim that God is created in our minds, we know God was not created, but that He chooses to live in our minds, heart, soul and spirit as we invite the only Immortal God into our hearts.

Darkness in our homes

In our homes we have issues, some are very visible, some are hidden and we often stray away from confronting these issues. They can seem very small or sometimes overwhelming, from parents who have an unruly child, living with a child that verbally and physically assaults you, to children that are emotionally and sexually assaulted by their parents/guardians. There are issues of incest in families, cousins sleeping with cousins, issues of whole families involved in crime. Where is the security of our homes?

There are the common problems of divorce, separation, and domestic violence. Where is the love in our homes?

Divorcing couples end up with situations where the child's emotions become confused and his/her loyalty becomes torn. We have high debt levels in our homes, because we have a borrowing culture, where we borrow to allow us to live above our means. Where is the wisdom in our homes?

Experts would open their mouth to speak about their varied analysis regarding the ills in our homes, the problems in our society, the corruption in our government. The list is endless and there is a myriad of supposing causative reasons why! Maybe the answer lies in looking back at what has taken place.

Many families no longer pray or eat together; there has been a steady decline in church membership in decades. The church has little say in government and politics; rather it has pressure put on it by government and politicians to keep its controversial ideas to itself and to take a seat in the congregation of the politically correct. There are various proposals for the scientist to have the final say on (when) life (begins) in regards to abortion, euthanasia and stem cell research. Over the last 300 years, scientists have already become the author of how the origins of the world came about, even though they were not present from the very beginning.

Just to put it plainly, the letter has been delivered to God. There is an ensign over the house of Lord and parliament saying 'God doesn't decide for us', the scientist hold up a banner that reads "We don't believe in God", the signs on our doors say 'I don't think you are needed here, God', our schools are making a poster for their gates 'God, keep out'. It is a wonder that the threats have not been attached to these signposts already or are they?

I believe the threats towards God, warning Him not to invade all these different areas of society are already present and could become more violent. We have spoken the 'Or else!' phrase more than once.

> *"And such as do wickedly against the covenant shall be corrupt by flatteries: but the people that do know their God shall be strong: and do exploits".*
>
> *(Daniel 11; 32)*

The spoken threats are the actions to ban Christians from evangelising on the streets. We can imagine society saying, 'God, if you dare to proclaim your-self in the streets after we've attempted to put a restraining order on you, we would put your followers in prison, we'll fine them'. They are further elaborated in attempts by the government to allow civil partnership to take place in churches. Breathing out even more violent threats, 'we know you said your house will be a house of prayer, but continue speaking out against homosexuality in our age and we would invade and violate your house, in fact we would defile your temple'.

In this hour of darkness, we can be tempted to despair just as Job was tempted to despair. We know that his story ended well, that his latter end was better than his former, and he had twice as much as he had before his calamity. We can believe with much assurance that our latter shall be better than the former. Therefore, all though I've mentioned a lot of ills that trouble us and our families, and the world we live in, we should not become disheartened, but rather rejoice at the darkness that seems to be so present at the moment, in the knowledge that a greater reward awaits us, and the greater glorification of God.

> *"For the arms of the wicked shall be broken: but the Lord upholdeth the righteous"*
>
> *(Psalm Ch.37 vv17).*

When God called Abraham to leave his family and the land of his father to go to a land that God would show him. God told him, *'... fear not, Abram: I am thy shield, and thy exceeding great reward' (Gen Ch.15 vv1).* In our choice to invite God into all aspects of our lives, and in choosing to obey Him, in the midst of this 'darkness', He speaks the same words unto us.

> *"When I was daily with you in the temple, ye stretched forth no hands against me: but this is your hour and the power of darkness."*
>
> *(Luke Ch.22 vv53)*

I suggest that there is an hour given to darkness, a time for darkness to prosper. Just as in the time of Jesus, when darkness was given an hour to demonstrate its power, which led to His arrest and death. Even now there is a time given for darkness to exercise its power, not that God is unaware, but rather a remonstration that God is in control.

As the church of God we hope and pray that the Kingdom of God should come. But do we resist this Kingdom by our actions? We pray Thy will be done! Do we resist His will? Not through our words but through our actions, when we find a way to have what we want despite what God said, when we prophesy or speak falsely in His name, are we not in rebellion?

In the book of Jeremiah, God promised to punish Shemaiah, and to cut off his seed and generation because he taught rebellion against the Lord. This was a time when Nebuchadnezzar had already carried away part of Israel and Judah into exile, because the Lord had caused them to go into captivity for their sins. The Lord had earlier sent his people in exile a word of comfort, telling them to build houses, marry wives and have children in the land of exile. That He would prosper them, God also urged them to seek the peace of the city to which they had been exiled, for in its peace they would have peace (Jeremiah Ch29 vv7). However Shemaiah claimed that the Lord had made him a priest, and urged the people not to listen to the prophecy that came out of Jeremiah's mouth and by his letter to the exiles.

This is what the Lord declared regarding Shemaiah:

"Send to them of the captivity, saying, Thus saith the Lord concerning Shemaiah the Nehelamite: Because that Shemaiah hath prophesied unto you, and I sent him not, and he caused you to trust in a lie: Therefore thus saith the Lord, Behold, I will punish Shemaiah the Nehelamite, and his seed: he shall not have a man to dwell among this people, neither shall he behold the good that I will do for my people, saith the Lord, because he hath taught rebellion against the Lord."

(Jeremiah Ch.29 vv31 – 32)

I am not only speaking about the darkness that lies out there in the world, or our families, but also about the darkness that is even closer; the darkness that lies within us. Have we identified the darkness in us, the areas of our lives which stand in rebellion against God? There is an urgency in the spirit, calling us to come into divine order, to come and reside at a place where our will starts to line up, and we start to submit our thoughts to Christ.

This darkness that lies within us can be typified by the result of the recent Ipso Moris Poll, in which 46% of UK Christians were against the idea of the UK having an official state religion, 38% of Christians opposed to the teaching of six-day creationism compared to 31% in support of its teaching in state schools. 36% of Christians opposing the daily act of Christian worship in state schools compared to 39% in favour of it, 62% of Christians in the poll were in support of women having an abortion within the legal limit, with just 20% against it, other results from the poll included.

According to the poll 26% of Christians completely believed in the power of prayer, while 21% either didn't completely believe it or didn't believe in it at all. 49% of Christians had not attended a church service apart from weddings, funerals and baptisms or such special occasions. Some 16% had not attended for 12 years, and a further 12% had never attended church.

This census was carried out in 2011, at least the Richard Dawkins foundation is right in one respect, secularism is rife not just in society at large, but even among those who call themselves Christians. The poll further showed that

54% of the public classified themselves as Christians compared to 72% in the 2001 census. Even Christians are lifting a banner against God, saying I know better, and I'm qualified to make every decision in my life despite your laws.

We have a promise from God, and I'm bold enough to say that God is permitting a time of captivity for His church, a time of oppression, an hour of darkness. However, just as in times past He shows us his power to deliver us from this present darkness, he demonstrates His power to reconcile us to Himself and continually pursues His glory as He manifests His purposes. Even as God has demonstrated before, when he allowed an hour of darkness in which Jesus Christ was crucified and mocked by sinners, but its result was His resurrection and the salvation of the world.

Making Firm Preparations

In my journey so far I have realized the need to be spiritually prepared. When we set out on a natural venture we make preparations. We save for the future, we have a pension fund for when we retire, we prepare our materials when we've got a presentation to make, we prepare for weddings, we prepare for funerals, we even get ready for church. When success is highly desirable or failure is too costly, lengthy and proper preparations are usually the norm.

There is an old adage that says 'proper preparation prevents poor performance'. In natural life this is very true. During my travels and as my time at medical school drew to a close I have been challenged with the idea of being spiritually prepared. As I've grown older I have felt I have constantly moved from a place of 'untested innocence' to a place where I had to choose whom to serve. I have had to make the decision on numerous occasions to maintain integrity and hold on to the truth in the face of temptation; some of these temptations and trials have been great.

I do recognise that I am not the only Christian who is making this transition. For we see ourselves getting rid of the list we keep of all the vile and immoral things that we have not done, but choosing to make a stand for the things that we believe in. Just like Joshua who declared, ' as for me and my house we will serve the Lord'. It is noteworthy that he made this declaration after God had given him and the children possession of most of the Promised Land and peace on every side.

> "And if it seem evil unto you to serve the Lord, choose you this day whom ye will serve: whether the gods which your fathers served that were on the other side of the flood, or the gods of the Amorites, in whose land ye dwell: but as for me and my house, we will serve the Lord".
>
> *(Joshua Ch.24 vv15)*

The time of ignorance when everyone did as she/he pleased has passed; the time of untested innocence will pass. It is the time of wilful choice, we are in such a conundrum that we know that the trials will come, the temptations will come, and sometimes they might seem very enormous.

But in the times of our testings and trials we have to make a choice every moment. At these points we can feel as though God is testing us at all times and marking our ways. Our emotions could bear some similarity to what Job felt although the context is different in this case.

> *"How many are mine iniquities and sins? Make me to know my transgression and my sin. Wherefore hidest thou thy face, and holdest me for thine enemy? Wilt thou break a leaf driven to and fro? And wilt thou pursue the dry stubble? For thou writest bitter things against me, and makest me to possess the iniquities of my youth. Thou puttest my feet also in the stocks, and lookest narrowly unto all my paths: thou settest a print upon the heels of my feet."*
>
> *(Job Ch.13 vv24-27)*

Like I've mentioned thus far, that at times the rebellion in our heart is not so overt. Its manifestations can be seen in the times when we are tested. If we don't prepare for the temptations and trials that await us in all the places where we go, the consequences are that we will fail to live a life that brings glory to God, as the things that trouble us are brought to the forefront. Take for example a man going into the mission fields alone, far away from his family. If he is to be away from his family for an extended period of time, he must count the cost that loneliness awaits him, and that perchance the enemy could test his resolve. If he takes note of this, then he can make plans either for his family to join him at some point or to return at an earlier point.

> *"If any man come to me, and hate not his father, and mother, and wife, and children, and brethren,*

and sisters, yea, and his own life also, he cannot be my disciple. And whosoever doth not bear his cross, and come after me, cannot be my disciple. For which of you, intending to build a tower, sitteth not down first, and counteth the cost, whether he has sufficient to finish it? Lest haply, after he hath laid the foundation, and is not able to finish it, all that behold it begin to mock him. Saying, this man began to build, and was not able to finish. Or what king, going to make war against another king, sitteth not down first, and consulteth whether he be able with ten thousand to meet him that cometh against him with twenty thousand? Or else while the other is yet a great way off, he sendeth an ambassage, and desireth conditions of peace. So likewise, whosoever he be of you that forsaketh not all that he hath, he cannot be my disciple."

(Luke Ch.14 vv26 – 33)

Preparing for our tests is essential; we must prepare to avoid shame and embarrassment. When we fail to pass our tests we become a joke and an embarrassment before our enemies. In preparing we must count the cost, whether it be the cost of living a life as a pastor or minister of God, the cost of being a missionary, the cost of being bold about our faith for Jesus in our work places. This is not about going the extra mile, Jesus makes it quite clear in the book of Luke, it is the minimum requirement!

To act with this knowledge in mind is to not be ignorant of the devil's devices. If we fail to prepare, then we prepare to be spiritual failures, unable to command the glory of

God in our lives, and in the earth because of an absence of obedience. In the context of this book, to prepare is to ask God to first reveal to us and then to address the hidden rebellions in our hearts. We can no longer afford to be spiritually naive. If we choose to remain naive, the enemy will fill our bellies with falsehood. And being pregnant with falsehood will stop us from being unable to conceive the truth of God.

All things Manifested in You

If I searched the whole of the world
I cannot find a love like yours
A love so pure and true
That its manifest in all things

You gave me life, love, hope and peace
Now I'm asking one thing
To give me the fruits of the spirit
That I might be manifest in you

I pray, goodness will never be far from me
But will abound, more graciously
Love from the heart
Longsuffering so enduring
That it might be manifest in me

There were those times, when I turned away
And felt that I could not feel you
Though that I knew your peace and
Grace abounded even more, and yet
My flesh was manifest in me

Gentleness be a part of my life
That I might show brotherly kindness
Faith and hope, to last eternity
Will you be manifest in me?

CHAPTER 9

Unstable Ground

In Daniel 2 verse 44, it is mentioned that the Kingdom of Christ shall not be left to other people, but it shall break in pieces and consume all these kingdoms, and it shall stand forever. Here we see God's kingdom in which there can be no mingling, put plainly it will not be mingled with the world; it will not be contaminated by the ideas of the kingdoms of this world. It is a kingdom that stands for ever and before whom all other kingdoms are vanquished.

I thought it important to highlight this truth about the kingdom that God has prepared for us to receive before venturing on to discuss why being unstable is a problem. As I realize that we have to be consistent in our obedience and submission unto Christ. So far I have talked about a covert rebellion in secret places, in our schools, in the shadow government, in our homes, in our hearts.

A rebellion led by men and women of renown, by a majority.

Our music icons, political figures, film stars all are pedalling ideas that challenge the order of God. I am not writing to you advocating a battle against these covert rebellions using human methods or weapons we can imagine, but a call to contest such rebellion with truth, integrity and righteousness. Having strength of numbers or men of renown behind us does not make us right, neither does it qualify us. Doing the right thing makes us right, and passing our tests qualifies us.

Restoration by water

I once attended a baptism of a man in his mid-forties, it so happened that him and his wife were being baptized on the same day. The testimony they gave was very moving, and truly encouraged me, reminding me of how it was when I first met the Lord. He had grown up in the church, and deeply loved the Lord as a teenager. As he grew in the church he was involved in the youth ministry and evangelism.

However while still in his mid-teens he left the church. He left because of certain happenings in the church, certain people in leadership had let the ministry down through their conduct and he felt not everyone was who they said they were; the nature of this unseemly conduct he didn't relate during his testimony. After he left the church he sort of drifted away from God, he didn't stop believing in God, but he knew he wasn't as close to God like he should be and even found it difficult to pray.

For thirty years he was away from God and away from church. In this time he got married and had two beautiful daughters, he built a very successful business and hence in most people's eyes he wasn't missing much at all. However despite his achievements after thirty years, plus having a beautiful wife and two gorgeous daughters, he still felt he was missing something. He described it as a void in himself that he couldn't fill with anything else but God.

He then visited a couple of churches where he lived, and started talking to friends about church and about God. Eventually he visited a particular church and felt when he got there he had come home (in his own words). He enrolled unto the 'alpha course'; through the course he was able to gain strength in his faith and to come to a better understanding and knowledge of who Jesus was to him. From the time he began chasing after God and seeking to return to the Father's house, he kept telling his wife to go with him. The end result being his wife also attended the alpha course and from being an unbeliever, in time she came to believe in the Lord Jesus. Later on they both made the decision to get baptized. This time, he had indeed come home.

Some of us might know people with stories like this; I particularly love this testimony. While giving his testimony he kept saying that he felt he had lost/wasted the last thirty years he spent away from God. I believe that God ministered to him and showed him he was in the restorative business, saving not only him but his wife as well, when he made his decision to turn back to God.

"And I will restore to you the years that the locust hath eaten, the cankerworm, and the caterpillar, and the palmerworm, my great army which I sent among you. And ye shall eat in plenty, and be satisfied, and praise the name of the Lord your God,

that hath dealth wondrously with you: and my people shall never be ashamed."

(Joel Ch.2 vv25 – 26)

The Lord is telling us He can restore all we've lost due to disobedience, due to our double-mindedness. He is able to give it all back and more when we choose to become stable. Isaiah chapter 26 says 'He will keep in perfect peace whose mind is stayed on Him'. It is His intent to restore us through his word, for we are indeed clean through the word that Christ Jesus has spoken to us. He is here to restore us in the spirit of baptism through the waters of baptism. Burying our sin and our guilty past, washing us and raising us up to new life through the power of His blood.

I find this story relevant, as in my own mind I could suggest some possible reason why he drifted away from God. Sometimes people leave a certain congregation but it doesn't mean that they left God. They remain disciples though they've moved on to fellowship in another congregation, in the scheme of things, this is irrelevant in relation to this discussion, as there is only one Chief shepherd. The intent of the Chief shepherd is to gather his sheep from all corners of the earth into one flock, not into a particular denomination.

Let's suppose that he drifted away from God because he had become what I would be calling unstable. So he was prone to change, not constant but fluctuating. Unstableness speaks of not being steady or firmly placed, perhaps even fickle. There are many things in life which are unstable; tides can be described as unstable. When used in relation to faith in Christ, this condition is more dangerous than a storm.

Being unstable as a believer, could equate to not being constant in your profession to be a Christian, fluctuating in your behaviour as a Christian, not remaining steady in relation to your faith in God's promises. It is allowing doubt in your mind; it is giving doubt a role in your walk with God. It is forgetting that Christ is the rock of your salvation, when you stand on a rock; you know you cannot be shaken.

I speak of being unstable as a rebellion, and I would entreat your permission to discuss this further. Let us look to the book of Genesis.

"Reuben, thou art my firstborn, my might and the beginning of my strength, the excellency of dignity, and the excellency of power. Unstable as water, thou shalt not excel, because thou wentest up to thy father's bed, then defiledst thou it: he went up to my couch."

(Gen Ch.49 vv3-4)

The meaning of these verses is powerful, in its beginning Jacob tells us of the excellency and dignity of his first born Reuben. What blessings he was bestowed with naturally as a consequence of being the first born and the beginning of Israel's strength. We see his dignity, for example in earlier verses, when Joseph's brother tried to kill him, he stopped them from killing him and allowed them to put him in a pit with the intent that he was going to save him later on. This he did because he was honourable and he didn't want to bring heartache to his father.

However, through the chapters of Genesis, we start to notice that despite his strength and power he was unstable. In that same story, we can perhaps see that if he wasn't unstable, he being the eldest and full of good intent, he could have withstood his brothers and told them that the folly and madness they were about to undertake was not permissible as it was evil, particularly for a family that knew the living God. This unstableness is further revealed when he sleeps with his father's concubine, Rachel's servant.

> *"And it came to pass, when Israel dwelt in that land, that Reuben went and lay with Bilhah his father's concubine, and Israel heard it. Now the sons of Jacob were twelve."*
>
> *(Gen Ch.35 vv22)*

Reuben should have known better, that it wasn't only unlawful, but actually it was an act that was an abomination before God. Meaning it was something that shouldn't have happened, because it was equivalent to him discovering his father's nakedness. In the Levitical laws, Moses expresses this quite clearly. Laws that were abomination were things like not having sexual intercourse with two sisters, not sleeping with a mother and daughter, not touching your father's wife (step-mother). It is interesting how these actions occur today and some people see nothing wrong in them. Paul in his epistle to the Corinthians spoke strongly against such abominable acts.

The result of Reuben's instability was that he would not excel. In order words he would not prosper. This is a lesson we can take from Reuben's history, if we are unstable as water we will not excel. As first born Reuben was supposed to be king over Israel, he was supposed to be leader among his brothers. This entitlement was transferred to Judah.

> *"The sceptre shall not depart from Judah, nor a lawgiver from between his feet: until Shiloh come: and unto him shall the gathering of the people be."*
> *(Gen Ch.49 vv10)*

Today we can look back and see the truth of Israel's prophecy, for after Saul was removed from being King; there was always a King over Judah and Jerusalem until after the death of Christ (Shiloh), unto whom the nations have been gathered by the power of His name. Even here we see God the father's plan to glorify the Son, and cause all nations to be saved and named in Him.

Now let us examine Judah.

> *"And Judah said unto his brethren. What profit is it if we slay our brother, and conceal his blood? Come, and let us sell him to the Ishmeelites, and let not our hand be upon him, for he is our brother and our flesh. And his brethren were content. Then there passed by Midianites merchantmen: and they drew and lifted up Joseph out of the pit, and sold Joseph to the Ishmeelites for twenty pieces of silver: and they brought Joseph to Egypt."*
> *(Gen Ch.37 vv26 – 29)*

Above we see Judah, as being very influential among his brothers. He made a decision and gives a reason for his decision, and his brothers listened to him, those that were older and those that were younger. When Reuben was absent, and the Ishmeelites per chance happened to be passing by, Judah thought it was better for them to sell Joseph than kill him

> *"And Judah acknowledged them and said, she hath been more righteous than I: because that I gave her not to Shelah my son. And he knew her again no more"*
> *(Gen Ch.38 vv26)*

The verse above refers to Judah's statement when he realized he was responsible for his daughter in-law, Tamar's pregnancy. In these verses we can see that Judah, despite not doing the right things initially, understood the law, so that he was able to give a good judgement on a matter. In Tamar's case, he realized he hadn't kept his word to her, so he was able to overturn his initial judgement of having her burnt, because he heard she had played the harlot (acted as a prostitute). He let her be, because she showed how he had broken his vow, which she had been waiting for.

Now let us return to Genesis chapter 49, verses 8–9:

> *"Judah, thou art he whom thy brethren shall praise: thy hand shall be in the neck of the enemies: thy father's children shall bow down before thee. Judah is a lion's whelp: from the prey, my son, thou art gone up: he stooped down, he couched as a lion and as an old lion, who shall rouse him up?"*

I believe that Judah was transformed over time to the person that he became at the time of Jacob's blessing. From an immoral man, who willingly sold his brother for money, to a man who could acknowledge the errors of his ways and accept sound judgement.

Now we are in a place where the stableness of our minds and the consistency of our character are important in determining our future and of the generation after us. No longer can we afford to be hot and cold, lest we be spewed out of the Lord's mouth (rejected by God). We are to make a decision either to be hot or cold (faithful or unfaithful), either to serve God or not. We should endeavour to encourage one another to become people who are consistent with our character, and whose behaviour is consistent with the words that they say.

One of the problems with the church throughout history is that at times the church tries to evolve to deal with the challenges thrown at it by the world, whether it is moral, scientific, or economical. The church needs to realize we do not need to react to the things around us, which would be mere human reasoning. Rather the answer lies in us being transformed into the image of Christ, if we hold this truth dear, we are sure to challenge the world we live in with the power and truth of the gospel.

"But we all, with open face beholding as in a glass the glory of the Lord, are changed into the same image from glory to glory, even as by the Spirit of the Lord"
(2 corinthians Ch.3 vv18).

CHAPTER 10

The Cure from the Hidden Rebellion

When treating medical conditions we commonly treat symptoms as well as the underlying cause. For example in asthma bronchodilators are given to relieve the symptom of airway tightness and acute shortness of breath, asthmatic patients also receive inhaled steroids to dampen down the inflammatory process causing asthma. Bronchodilators open the windpipe and lower airways, making it easier to breathe. Let's consider another condition, systemic lupus erythematosus (SLE). This is an autoimmune disease which can affect any organ in the body, in layman terms the autoimmune process is brought about by the body's immune cells attacking other cells of the body inappropriately.

SLE can affect the joints, causing joint pain and destruction. The pain is a symptom of the underlying process causing the joint destruction. Doctors prescribe analgesics (pain killers) to kill the pain, but depending on the severity of the disease, stronger drugs which are disease modifying agents (DMARDs) are used to control the underlying autoimmune inflammatory process. Diseases like this tend to increase in severity with time in a significant majority of patients without treatment.

We can liken this to the hidden rebellions of our hearts

which are not overt. We can choose to just treat the symptoms and live unhappy unfulfilled lives, or we can find a cure for the underlying cause (which lies in the heart in this case). The problem of our rebellion comes from our inappropriate desires and wrongful thought patterns. Without addressing these matters of the spiritual heart, these rebellions grow and mature into tumours and can then metastasize affecting other organs of our body (other aspects of our life). It is true that treating a disease with the wrong medicine won't work, the same way we have noted in ourselves that we have failed to rid ourselves of some rebellious habits despite our efforts.

Perhaps we've been applying the wrong balm; we have been taking the wrong medicine, so that there has been no healing. You can put a thief in prison and he will not steal for the duration that he is in prison, but the minute he is let out he is found stealing again. At times I feel I've come to this point, and I confess that I am of little strength and can do nothing of myself, 'gye nyame' (except God).

> *"I hurt with the hurt of my people. I mourn and am overcome with grief. Is there no medicine in Gilead? Is there no physician there? Why is there no healing for the wounds of my people?"*
> *(Jeremiah 8 vv21 - 22 New living translation (NLT)*

Rebellion cannot exist within the kingdom of God; he that must enter must have child-like faith. He/she must recognise that I do not know everything or understand everything to allow myself to have the final authority over my life, so I must leave it to the one person that does (aka God). Your sin and rebellion will not cause God to abandon you, because God is gracious and is interested in reconciling the rebellious child back to Himself.

– Keys for overcoming the hidden rebellion:

* *Trust*

> *"And Moses lifted up his hand, and with his rod he smote the rock twice: and the water came out abundantly, and the congregation drank, and their beasts also: And the Lord spoke unto Moses and Aaron. Because ye believed me not, to sanctify me in the eyes of the children of Israel, therefore ye shall not bring this congregation into the land I have given them. This is the water of Meribah: because the children of Israel strove with the Lord, and He was sanctified in them."*
>
> *(Numbers Ch.20 vv11 – 13)*

In the above passage, Moses was grieved because his eyes were focused on how weak he was, when the children of Israel asked for water in the wilderness. Can you identify with this? There have been many situations that have made me feel very inadequate, and I didn't keep my eyes on God.

> *"And now, O Lord God, thou art that God and thy words be true, and thou hast promised this goodness unto thy servant."*
>
> *(2 Samuel Ch.7 vv28)*

> *"Stand in awe, and sin not: commune with your own heart upon your bed, and be still, selah. Offer*

the sacrifices of righteousness, and put your trust in the Lord. There be many that say, who will show us any good? Lord, lift thou up the light of thy countenance upon us."

(Psalm Ch.4 vv4-6)

- Surrender to God

- Moving away from self-centredness to Christ centeredness

- When faced with rebellious people, do not react but act in the position of your designated authority

- Turning towards God

- Have confidence as you operate in your God given authority

- Having a child-like faith – as God is qualified to have the final authority in your life. He that must enter the kingdom of God must have a child-like faith. He/she must recognise that I do not know everything, or understand everything to allow myself to have the final authority over my life, so I must leave it to the one person that does.

- Do not resort to human help, but turn to God

Autoimmune diseases are conditions that can be treated with long term suppression of the immune system. Our tendency to turn away or rebel from God is not an acute problem, but a chronic condition, due to the conflict between our old nature which is natural to us, and the new nature which we receive in Christ Jesus, by being born of water and the Spirit of God. The Holy Spirit who is the presence of God in our lives, heart and in all the earth is the balm that we need to be embalmed in, wrapped in, in order for us to remain in a state of remission from our hidden rebellions. Only a heart that is broken and continually yielded to God can enjoy the spiritual prosperity that King Hezekiah enjoyed, in that he prospered wherever he went because he cleaved and clung unto God.

The Great Stone

The Kingdom of God will surely come and all His words of truth will surely be fulfilled. The spirit of God is speaking to us in these times to choose life, to choose freedom and peace. Truly the eyes of the Lord has gone over the face of the earth and has seen that there is none that continually does good, there is none that is righteous. His plans are so intricate that the things which seem impossible in our eyes are possible with Him. He invites us to his granary (storehouse).

> *Isaiah 28;*
> *27For the dill is not threshed with a threshing instrument, neither is a cart wheel turned about upon the cummin; but the dill is beaten out with a staff and the cummin with a rod.*
>
> *28Bread corn is beaten, because he will not ever be threshing it, nor break it with the wheel of his cart,*

nor bruise it with his horsemen.

29This also cometh forth from the LORD of hosts, who is wonderful in counsel and excellent in working.

These verses show us that God knows just what to do to get the desired results from us, to make us as fine as we should be. The process all starts with being broken, it is allowing God to apply pressure on us and responding as He desires. In coming to His granary, He will cause us to be threshed or beaten as required.

In Daniel chapter 2, we see an encapsulation of the beginning and ending of all human authority, powers and dominions. We've had different world powers at the different times, they lasted for a time and then they crumbled. We've had the Babylonian empire, the Persian empire, the Roman empire. We know of when Britain was a world superpower and now when America is the world's super power. These entire kingdoms rose up for a season and then their kingdom was brought to nothing. There is a God that knows the beginning and the end, His name is 'Alpha and Omega'.

"But there is a God in heaven that revealeth secrets, and maketh known to the King Nebuchadnezzar what shall be in the latter days. Thy dreams, and the visions of thy head upon thy bed, are these; As for thee, O king, thy thoughts came into thy mind upon thy bed, and what should come to pass hereafter: and he that revealeth secrets maketh known to thee what shall come to pass. But as for

me, this secret is not revealed to me for any wisdom
that I have more than any living, but for their sakes
that shall make known the interpretation to the
king, and that thou mightiest know the thoughts of
thy heart"

(Daniel Ch.2 vv28 – 30)

Nebuchadnezzar revealed this prophetic dream for a reason, he needed to know its interpretation and it wasn't God's will for the wise men and magicians and diviners of Babylon to die. God is challenging us, the words that He has spoken to us; the visions He has given us are because we have a generation to serve and a purpose to accomplish for His glory.

He wants to put us to His use and give fulfilments to our hearts, like I've mentioned earlier in respect to John Piper's quote: 'God is most glorified when we are most satisfied in Him'.

Let us explore this story further, as we come to the important part of the passage. Verses 31–35:

"Thou, O king, sawest, and behold a great image.
This great image, whose brightness was excellent,
stood before thee: and the form thereof was terrible.
This image's head was of fine gold, his breast and
his arms of silver, his belly and his thigh of brass.
His legs of iron, his feet part of iron and part of clay.
Thou sawest till that a stone was cut out without
hands, which smote the image upon his feet that
were of iron and clay, and brake them to pieces.
Then was the iron, the clay, the brass, the silver, and
the gold, broken to pieces together, and became like

the chaff of the summer threshing floors; and the wind carried them away, that no place was found for them: and the stone that smote the image became a great mountain, and filled the earth."

Here we see a stone that smote the feet of the statue, the feet which represented an empire that was part strong and part week, which was the last of the empires before the stone appeared.

(Verses 40 – 42) "And the fourth kingdom shall be strong as iron: forasmuch as iron breaketh in pieces and subdueth all things: and as iron that breaketh all these, shall it break in pieces and bruise. And whereas thou sawest the feet and toes, part of potters' clay, and part of iron, the kingdom shall be divided: but there shall be in it of the strength of the iron, forasmuch as thou sawest the iron mixed with miry clay. And as the toes of the feet were part of iron, and part of clay, so the kingdom shall be partly strong and partly broken."

In verse 44, there is the announcement of Christ's arrival and Him establishing a kingdom which can never be destroyed.

"And in the days of these kings shall the God of heaven set up a kingdom, which shall never be destroyed: and the kingdom shall not be left to other people, but it shall break in pieces and consume all these kingdoms, and it shall stand for ever".

The message I'm bringing is that our healing starts the

moment we fall upon this stone (Christ). For whoever falls upon this stone will be broken, and it is good that we should be broken, because then we know the potters hands can make us into a vessel that is fit for His purpose, but if we continually resist, we'll be on the other side. As we can see, whomsoever the stone falls upon will be crushed, as we see from the visions of Nebuchadnezzar. We have received a letter from God (in His word) inviting us to be broken and healed, and to escape being crushed and destroyed by the stone. This is the same stone that the builder's rejected, who at that time did not recognize Him as the Chief corner stone, the one who fills all the earth (even Christ Jesus).

> " Forasmuch as thou sawest that the stone was cut out of the mountain without hands, and that it brake in pieces the iron, the brass, the clay, the silver, and the gold; the great God hath made known to the king what shall come to pass hereafter: and the dream is certain, and the interpretation thereof sure."
> (Daniel Ch.2 vv45)

The heart of the Father

> "And when he came to himself, he said, How many hired servants of my father's have bread enough and to spare, and I perish with hunger! I will arise and go to my father, and will say unto him, Father, I have sinned against heaven, and before thee; and am no more worthy to be called thy son. But the father said to his servants, bring forth the best robe, and put it on him: and put a ring on his hand, and

*shoes on his feet, and bring hither the fatted calf,
and kill it: and let us eat, and be merry. For this my
son was dead, and is alive again: he was lost, and is
found. And they began to be merry"*

(Luke Ch.15 vv17 – 24)

The Father says "everything I have is yours". Our minds
should view our lives in a way that understands that the
Father is not interested as such in our success or what we
achieve in this life, as such as in the person we become, for
He says everything I have is yours, you are my son. Our
sin and rebellion does not cause God to abandon us.

His plans are of reconciliation, drawing our rebellious
heart back to Him, because He treasures our sonship, He
longs that we might not leave His abode, that we would
not forsake His family. If we do stray, He waits, looking
afar off, lifting His eyes into the distance to behold our
home coming, our return. Then He runs towards us with
arms that were stretched out wide on the cross of Calvary.
He clothes us with His blood (purple robe), guaranteeing
our royal priesthood and giving us access into the Throne
room. He puts a ring on our finger (giving us dominion,
power and authority), that we would sit and rule and
judge with Him.

We feel ill treated, unfairly treated, disregarded,
unacknowledged as sons. Our hearts cry 'Father this long
have I been with you and I have served you, yet you have
not clothed me with a new robe, you have not put a ring
on my finger, you have not thrown a party for me, you
have not celebrated me. He replies "you are my son, you
are always on my mind, because I hold you in such regard

and I'm zealous for your good, all that I have is yours"; He says "abide with me always. You are already dressed in my garments, my ring is yours, I your father celebrate you always because I'm in the business of preparing you to receive the Kingdom, as you have been with me always."

> *"Now his elder son was in the field: and as he came and drew nigh to the house, he heard musick and dancing. And he called one of the servants, and asked what these things meant. And he said unto him, Thy brother is come: and thy father hath killed the fatted calf, because he hath received him safe and sound. And he was angry, and would not go in: therefore came his father out, and entreated him. And he answering said to his father, Lo, these many years do I serve thee, neither transgressed I at any time thy commandment: and yet thou never gavest me a kid, that I might make merry with my friends: But as soon as this thy son was come, which hath devoured thy living with harlots, thou hast killed for him the fatted calf. And he said unto him, Son, thou art ever with me, and all that I have is thine. It was meet that we should make merry, and be glad: for this thy brother was dead, and is alive again: and was lost, and is found."*
>
> *(Luke Ch.15 vv25 – 32)*

In the heart of the father, the elder son is not abandoned neither is the younger son forgotten. Even when the elder son is tempted to be rebellious in heart, the father comes to Him and makes peace, saying come back into the house, and be not afar off. Return into that close fellowship where you know my heart, so you can truly see, believe, know for yourself, that all I have is yours and you are beloved. The father is interested in bringing all hearts back to Himself, no matter how far they've drifted; all He awaits is for us to cease from a heart of rebellion. This rebellion can exist while we're in the house, or when we are away from it, the Father is able to recognise it. He has the cure for it, for He is the balm in Gilead, and in all the earth. "The earth is the Lord's and the fullness thereof, the world and they that dwell therein." (Ps 24; 1)

Conclusions

• Rebellion results from a failure to be content with what God has given you

• It lies in self-centredness

• Rebellion twists the truth of God and exchanges it for a lie, usually based upon a past experience. For example "Is it a small thing that thou hast brought us up out of a land that floweth with milk and honey, to kill us in the wilderness, except thou make thyself a prince over us? Moreover thou hast not brought us into a land that floweth with milk and honey, or given us inheritance of fields and vineyards; wilt thou put out the eyes of these men? We will not come up" (Numbers Ch16 vv13 – 14). Here Korah and his companions lie against the promise of God, calling Egypt from which they were delivered a land flowing with milk and honey, and saying that God hath not brought them into such a land, when God had said I'm taking you from the land of bondage into a land flowing with milk and honey.

- Rebellion is revealed by the presence of God, implying rebellion can be hidden when we are away and fail to abide in the presence of God (Numbers Ch.16 vv24)

- Run away from people who start rebellion lest you be consumed in their sins (Numbers Ch.16 vv24 – 27)

"Harden not your heart, as in the provocation, and as in the day of temptation in the wilderness; when your fathers tempted me, proved me, and saw my work. Forty years long was I grieved with this generation, and said, it is a people that do err in their heart, and they have not known my ways: Unto whom I sware in my wrath that they should not enter into my rest."

(Psalm Ch.95 vv8 – 11)

I pray that God will deal with us as a father does, so that we will partake of the rest He has prepared for us. And that we would not be like Jonah at the beginning of this book who didn't realize he was a son and everything the master had was his, as long as he waited for the time of inheritance.

CHAPTER 11

The Bondservant

"Paul and Timotheus, the servants of Jesus Christ. To all the saints in Christ Jesus which are at Philippi, with the bishops and deacons."
(Phillipians Ch1 vv1)

To be sold out to someone is to be totally committed to the person in regardless to the circumstances or to any change in circumstances. The best definition I can think of for being sold out is found in the bible, which describes a bond servant. This is the equivalence of being a slave, however not a slave due to outward compulsion as in the case of the 'slave trade', but a willing slave. In the film 'The Count of Monte Cristo', we see the pirate whose life is spared by the star character of the film 'Edmond Dunston', vowing his allegiance and service to Edmond, due to Edmonds graciousness in sparing his life, he willingly gives his life in service to Edmond. This also is the calling of our Christian faith, in knowing the grace of God, in that God died for us, we also can lay down our own lives.

According to the dictionary, 'a slave' is a person who is owned by someone, or someone entirely dominated by some influence or person. The word bond is described as a connection that fastens things together, a restraint that confines or restricts freedom (especially used to tie down or restrain a prisoner), the property of sticking together (as of glue and wood) or the joining of surfaces of different composition, or it could be defined as a connection based on kinship or marriage or common interest.

Oswald Chambers in his daily devotional defines it as ' the breaking and collapse of my independence brought about by my own hands, and the surrendering of my life to the supremacy of the Lord Jesus.' He further goes on to clarify ' no one can do this for me, I must do it myself. God may bring me up to this point three hundred and sixty-five times a year, but He cannot push me through it. It means breaking the hard outer layer of my individual independence from God, and the liberating of myself and my nature into oneness with Him; not following my own ideas, but choosing absolute loyalty to Jesus'. For a further deliberation of this subject see Oswald Chamber's book, 'My Utmost for His highest'.

When I think of the phrase "bond servant", there are a few missionaries that come to mind. Mother Teresa, the Roman Catholic nun who obtained Indian citizenship so that she could serve the poor people in India. At the age of 18, she left her mother and sister to embark on a life as a missionary; she never saw them again after she left. In September of 1946 she describes what she coins ' the call within the call', while travelling to the convent. "I was to leave the convent and help the poor while living among them. It was an order. To fail would have been to break the faith."

Yet in her first year out on the streets living with and

helping the poor, she was faced with such difficulties that she was tempted to return to the convent. Her reply to this temptation was "... of free choice, my God, and out of love for you, I desire to remain and do whatever your Holy will in my regard." She stated she did not shed a single tear despite her feelings. So she founded the missionaries of charity in Calcutta in 1950, and for over 45years, she ministered to the poor, sick, orphaned and the dying.

Looking back at her work, one of the phrases which she used (which is my personal favourite), is. "The Lord has no hands but ours, the Lord has no feet but ours." There is so much understanding in this phrase, there is a true belief that God has a specific purpose for us, and the acceptance of such a truth staggers my mind. When I consider what it would mean and what it would cost to truly be God's hands and feet, and mouth-piece in this earth.

In 1867, a missionary minister, Reverend Thomas Baker from Sussex England, was killed in the Fiji Island. He was the last missionary to be martyred by cannibalism on the island. He was sent to the missionary field of Daveulevu in 1859. He led a party to spread the gospel in the heathen interior of Viti Levu, the mission ended with him being killed along with seven other Fijian Christian workers. Two men escaped the massacre. It is alleged that, when warned of a possible plot against his missionary party, he replied in Fijian that "sa yawa vei au ko Davuilevu, ka sa voleka vei au ko lomalagi". Translated it means, "Davuilevu is yet far, heaven for me is closer". Reverend Baker and his colleagues were killed on July 21, 1867.

Having the heart of a bond servant requires having an understanding of God's purpose for you, and having your eyes transfixed on the price, which is to gain Christ. It is knowing despite being under a far better covenant which is far better than the covenant based on the Mosaic law, its requirements are higher.

Joshua wasn't a priest, he was a warrior, but he dwelt where the priest was supposed to, before the ark of the covenant of God.

> *"And Joshua the son of Nun was full of the spirit of wisdom, for Moses had laid his hands upon him: and the children of Israel hearkened unto him, and did as the Lord commanded Moses".*
>
> *(Deuteronomy Ch.34 vv9)*

I have so far, beckoned to you the reader, as the spirit of God has beckoned to my heart. To come out of my rebellion, in stepping out of our rebellion, we are presenting ourselves before the altar of God. We come to the place where we prepare to offer a sacrifice and lay down our lives on the altar of total surrender to Elohim (God).

- The altar is made to burn incense on (offer praise)
  "By him therefore let us offer the sacrifice of praise to God continually, that is, the fruit of our lips, giving thanks to his name."

  (Hebrews Ch.13 vv15)

- It is a place of worship, it is the place of tithing
  "And Jacob rose up early in the morning and took

the stone that he had put for his pillows, and set it up for a pillar, and poured oil upon the top of it. And he called the name of that place Beth-el: but the name of that city was called Luz at the first. And Jacob vowed a vow, saying, if God will be with me, and will keep me in this way that I go, and will give me bread to eat, and raiment to put on, so that I come again to my father's house in peace, then shall the Lord be my God: And this stone, which I have set for a pillar shall be God's house; and of all that thou shalt give me I will surely give the tenth unto thee."
(Genesis Ch.28 vv18 -22)

- The altar is a place of establishing covenant
  "And the angel of the Lord called unto Abraham out of heaven the second time. And said, By myself have I sworn, saith the Lord, for because thou hast done this thing, and hast not withheld thy son, thine only son, that in blessing I will bless thee, and in multiplying I will multiply thy seed as the stars of the heaven, and as the sand which is upon the sea shore: and thy seed shall possess the gate of his enemies: And in thy seed shall all the nations of the earth be blessed: because thou hast obeyed my voice."
  (Gen Ch.22 vv15 – 18)

- We are to bring everything before the altar. When we build our altar we know what to do, we receive instructions on which battles to fight and which battles not to fight.

- At the altar we can bring all our sacrifices and offerings unto God.

The jealousy offering (Numbers Ch.5), Sin offering, harvest offering, thanksgiving offering, memorial offering, atonement offering

- It is a place where we declare our obedience, where we lay down our will

- Where we slay the things that are precious to us, (Genesis Ch.22 vv6-18)

- The place of receiving the Abrahamic promises

- A place of divine supply – for he called the name of that place Jehovah Jireh, that is in the mountain of the Lord it shall be seen

- It is the place where we see God's provision for us and not what we have provided ourselves

- Where we give what we cannot keep to gain what we cannot lose.
  "And when he had called the people unto him with his disciples also, he said unto them, whosoever will come after me, let him deny himself, and take up his cross, and follow me. For whosoever will save his life shall lose it; but whosoever shall lose his life for my sake and the gospel's, the same shall save it. For what shall it profit a man, if he shall gain the whole world, and lose his own soul? Or what shall a man give in exchange for his soul?"
  (Mark Ch.8 vv34 – 37)

- The altar can also speak of suffering.

Through various new testament accounts we learn that as we partake in the fellowship of Christ suffering, we can be sure that we would partake in the fellowship of His glory.

"For our light affliction; which is but for a moment, worketh for us a far more exceeding and eternal weight of glory; while we look not at the things which are seen, but at the things which are not seen: for the things which are seen are temporal; but the things which are not seen are eternal."

(2 Corinthians Ch.4 vv17-18)

Consequences of not building our altar

- Being out of fellowship with God

- Lack of accurate direction

- Weakness and vulnerability to the enemy

- Susceptibility to falling to temptation as we are drawn away by our own lust

- Inability to hear from God

- Difficulty worshipping/praising

- We become easily shaken and displaced from our position

- Our faith is shaken and we become unsure of who we

are, without the assurance of our identity we lack power

An immoral heart is an obstruction from setting up your altar; it is synonymous with those that want the blessings of the altar, but not the fellowship.

> *"Now of the things which we have spoken this is the sum: We have such an high priest who is at on the right hand of the throne of the Majesty in the heavens; A minister of the sanctuary, and of the true tabernacle, which the Lord pitched, and not man. For every high priest is ordained to offer gifts and sacrifices: wherefore it is of necessity that the man have somewhat also to offer. For if he were on earth, he should not be a priest, seeing that there are priests that offer gifts according to the law."*
>
> *(Hebrews Ch.8 vv1-4)*

In conclusion, the price to pay for our rebellions, no matter how little or how great is not worth it. Whether it involves dabbling with the occult which is witch craft, involving one's self in tarot card reading, believing and inclining your ears to what the horoscopes say. These are demonic voices posed as voices of men and women, giving us an expectation that is not based on God's word to us. Or it could be rebellion towards Godly ordained authority and principles. It is time to lay these rebellions down at the foot of God's altar, and allow God to take us on our journey of brokenness, that through the fellowship of His sufferings, He would bring us through a glorious vessel, declaring His marvellous acts.

Lord here I am again. I'm sorry, I promised You never to do it again but here I'm in my own mess. How can I go on, it seems I can't get out of this cycle no matter how hard I tried. Church was great last week... when I heard Your word I was ready to give everything for You ... but here I am again, please deliver *me*.

> *"Of them the proverbs are true: "A dog returns to its vomit, "[a]and, "A sow that is washed goes back to her wallowing in the mud."*
>
> *(2 Peter Ch.2 vv22)*

I cannot go on living my life for myself, Oh Lord it is too empty. I cannot go back to where I was before because Lord, I have tasted that you are good. I'm sorry Lord that I strayed away, now I'm back at Your gates, I've returned to my senses.

Hosea 2;
" *7 She will chase after her lovers but not catch them;*
she will look for them but not find them.
Then she will say,
'I will go back to my husband as at first,
for then I was better off than now.'

8 She has not acknowledged that I was the one
who gave her the grain, the new wine and oil,
who lavished on her the silver and gold—
which they used for Baal."

Forgive me Lord. Release me from the chains of Egypt,

that I might go to the place of Your choosing to offer a sacrifice to my God. In You is all my hope!

"How long, O LORD, must I call for help,
but you do not listen?
Or cry out to you, "Violence!"
but you do not save?" (Habukkuk Ch.1 vv2)

"I will stand at my watch
and station myself on the ramparts;
I will look to see what he will say to me,
and what answer I am to give to this complaint."
(Habukkuk Ch.2 vv1)

Bring reconciliation to my life and help me to live distinctly different from now on.

(Isaiah Ch.12)
¹ In that day you will say:
"I will praise you, O LORD.
Although you were angry with me,
your anger has turned away
and you have comforted me.

² Surely God is my salvation;
I will trust and not be afraid.
The LORD, the LORD, is my strength and my song;
he has become my salvation."

³ With joy you will draw water
from the wells of salvation."